THE POWER OF SEVEN IN MARKETING

Engaging Your Potential Customers

FARIS ALAMI

The Power of Seven in Marketing
Published by Faris Alami
USA

For book ordering, please visit the website:
www.myisminc.com

All quotes introducing chapters are from Faris Alami's blog on Medium at https://farisalami.medium.com

Alami, Faris
The Power of Seven in Marketing

ISBN 978-1-948723-12-1

The Power of Seven in Marketing

FARIS ALAMI

faris.alami@myisminc.com

www.myisminc.com

TABLE OF CONTENTS

SPECIAL THANKS

As I write this book, I realize it's been in process for at least two decades. After years of being in business for myself, and of assisting both small and large companies and institutions through International Strategic Management (ISM), in the early 2000s I began blogging every week about entrepreneurship, leadership, and globalization. Blogging became a platform whereby I could fine-tune what I was learning from my business results and the best practices of others.

Of course, throughout my years of blogging, I've benefited from all the wonderful people who have given me feedback, both good and bad, and I'm grateful for it. My exchanges with readers have helped me to grow tremendously!

I also developed a podcast and a YouTube channel to speak with everyday entrepreneurs about their experiences. I'm grateful for the interaction with people across every platform, not to mention the times I've met people at conferences, restaurants, and even airports. Each conversation has shown me how richly multi-layered the world of business is. In addition, during the past two years I've spent over fifty-eight hours every week on Zoom! Which means I've learned a great deal from over 5,000 people in over sixty countries.

Entrepreneurs worldwide have much to teach each other about pursuing relationships with people, nurturing customers, giving back to communities, and building businesses that endure. I hope this book impacts your entrepreneurial journey, and I would love to hear your thoughts and the results you achieve.

None of this would have been possible without my wife's support. Lara is an amazing soul and has been a pillar in my life that has kept me standing. My children's love and support also keep me going, along with the strong foundations provided by my mom, dad, and my extended family of aunts, uncles, cousins, parents-in-law, and all my friends and supporters throughout the years.

Thanks to all of you for your support and for reading. I am honored and humbled.

INTRODUCTION

Many entrepreneurs flounder in the first weeks, months, and years of their business because their customer base dwindles and never grows. After peddling their products and services to family and friends, they're at a loss what to do next. They experiment with expensive marketing campaigns and overhaul their business without thinking through their sales processes, all the while doubting why they became entrepreneurs in the first place.

What I've learned is that *intentional and frequent engagement* reaches customers. It takes time and a laser-sharp focus that studies customer behaviors and preferences, provides consistent messaging about products and services, practices considerate interaction with customers, and plans marketing and sales activities.

What I share in this book, and in my presentations across the world, I have drawn from the ups and downs in my life as an entrepreneur. I have also obtained insights and best practices from the thousands of outstanding entrepreneurs I've worked with over many years. Which doesn't mean I don't face challenges now: it just means this is what I have learned so far!

Business success isn't random: it's focused and measurable. You will face challenging times during your entrepreneurial journey. Although there will be moments when you will have to reimagine how you work, especially during a crisis, what will remain constant will be the chance to build a resilient foundation for success. As you can imagine, in my Resilient Entrepreneur Canvas, I work with leaders and entrepreneurs on how to overcome the challenges they face, and in this book we discuss the strategies you may need to deploy to maintain relationships that can support you during both good and bad times.

I developed 7-7-7 Marketing to provide a useful method that covers the successful strategies, tactics, and action steps I have seen and implemented throughout the years in order to engage customers, accelerate profits, and achieve long-term success. 7-7-7 Marketing addresses the multiple relational contacts or touches required to reach a customer, make a sale, and sustain a human connection.

As a young entrepreneur, I discovered a pattern: for every ten encounters I had with a customer, it was highly likely that this customer would purchase from me. Your averages may differ from mine, but I believe you will discover that intentional engagement pays off every time. I invite you to consider adding 7-7-7 Marketing to your business activities toolkit. While it's not the only tool you need, you'll see that the practices outlined in this book have helped my business and thousands of others—from startups to multi-million-dollar firms.

But sales advice is available everywhere, right? YouTubers teach about pitching customers. Bestselling Books on Amazon offer a cornucopia of sales help. What makes 7-7-7 Marketing different? And why should you trust me to support you? I will leave that up to you to figure out. But remember: what you get out of it will be what you put into it. So please dive in and try new things—even if it feels uncomfortable at the outset.

I've been fortunate in seeing my entrepreneurial journey blossom when I learned the fundamentals of sincerely engaging customers to make a sale. As I've always said, "no sales, no business." Sometimes it took more engagement with customers to make a sale; sometimes it took less. Nevertheless, each time I engaged with potential customers I learned a business lesson.

One of my most memorable lessons occurred when I was a teenager. In late 1990, I was a straight-A student in Kuwait on my way to Canada. I was lucky because throughout my entire school education, there was no question of my coming in second or third. It was like, "You're going to be at the top of the class—and that's all there is to it. Since we don't have passports, your passport will be your degree: it will open doors and take you places!"

That's what my parents told me, that's what my friends told me, and that's what I saw others do. And it's exactly what I ended up doing because I emulated the discipline of excellence and achievement demonstrated by my family members. Summers were spent studying for the following year.

Am I saying I never made mistakes or encountered challenges? I remember playing world football (soccer) early one morning. My downstairs neighbor had asked me not to hit the walls in the backyard of our apartment complex during those hours. However, the best time for football practice was at 6:00 or 7:00 a.m., so I ignored my neighbor's request.

After a few shouts from the neighbor's house, my friend's mom ran after me, grabbed the ball and took it away. She then threw it back to me—after running knife through it. Let's just say I had my own challenges to overcome!

Despite some poor decisions, such as that one, I focused on the educational path set out for me. I applied to both McGill University and Concordia University in Montreal, Quebec to study electrical and computer engineering. My father planned to join me on the trip, as he wanted to speak to our lawyer about immigrating to Canada. My entire family was excited, as Canada offered us the opportunity to find a new home.

We were scheduled to obtain an approved visa at a 2:00 p.m. appointment on August 2, 1990, at the Canadian embassy. But before we could reach the embassy, Saddam Hussein's forces invaded Kuwait early that morning, claiming that Kuwait belonged to his country.[1] A few days later, Kuwait became the nineteenth province of the Republic of Iraq, Hussein defending Iraq's claim on Kuwait based on boundaries dating back to the Ottoman Empire.[2]

The invasion devastated thousands of families, and many people lost their lives during the ensuing war. The invasion also upturned my family's life in Kuwait, along with my plans for college.

I remember my grandfather and grandmother telling me, "You're not going anywhere: the embassy is closed."

I also remember my reply. "We'll see."

Despite the gathering turmoil, my hopes and ambitions hadn't dimmed. I don't quite know why. Maybe it was my mindset. Maybe it was my youth that kept me hopeful. While Iraq dropped bombs as early as 5:00 a.m., by 9:00 a.m. the tanks were rolling past us in the streets. As they did, I waited at the front door, looking onto the street to see what was happening. The invasion instantly changed our world. The Kuwaiti government collapsed. We became residents of a place that didn't exist, an experience similar to that of my parents and grandparents in Palestine.

We lived in Kuwait on my dad's work permit, which was renewed every year. Although born in Kuwait, I was Palestinian. I carried the documents of a Palestinian refugee lived accordingly. But I belonged to occupied Palestine, where we traveled every summer for extended visits. Looking at family photos, you would never know we were refugees—and we considered ourselves very lucky not to live in a refugee camp.

My mother was born in Be'er Sheva in the Negev desert (Palestine, 1948); my father was born in Gaza (Palestine, 1948). In addition, they weren't in Gaza during the Six-Day War in 1967 when Israel took over Gaza from Egyptian control. As a result, the war prevented my family from returning to their relatives, homes, livelihoods, and the land they owned in 1948 and 1967.

Under Kuwaiti law, my family held work status and carried a refugee travel document issued by Egypt to Palestinians. However, my family detested the term 'refugee' to the point of never uttering it. Although we followed the rules outlined for refugees, within the privacy of our apartment in Kuwait, we often spoke of returning home to Gaza and of our dreams of visiting the old homes left behind in Palestine in 1948.

In the early days of the invasion, Ahmed, my high school teacher, called and said he had keys to the grocery store plaza. The government-run grocery stores in Kuwait offered a central place for buying and selling goods and services, such as groceries, shoe repair, hair salons, and dry cleaning. Losing access to those services created a huge resource gap for communities.

Defying Iraq's occupation, the Kuwaitis attempted to maintain the lifestyle they had enjoyed prior to the invasion. It was a dangerous undertaking. Kuwaitis couldn't be too visible during the Iraqi occupation or they risked being tortured. They couldn't operate a prominent grocery store and work with suppliers during wartime. My teacher believed that the best way to protect resources was through a student he trusted. Hopefully, that student wouldn't attract as much attention because he was Palestinian, not Kuwaiti.

That student was me. I was eighteen years old.

When my teacher gave me the grocery store plaza keys, he instructed me to hire employees, keep the money safe, and ensure that the invasion hadn't disrupted the supply chain. (Anyone who has lived through wartime or even COVID-19 knows that the supply chain gets hit first! No one wants to risk their life going to work, and the supplies and distribution channels become disrupted.)

My teacher told me, "I'll give you all the phone numbers for the supply companies because they're all operating now. You might start by seeing if you can refurbish some things you're selling."

The grocery store was upstairs. When you walked about one hundred steps down, you reached the police station, which the Iraqi soldiers had seized. Every day they detained me for questioning because I had the keys. The Iraqi soldiers quizzed me often: "How did you get the keys?" "How do you obtain the supplies? How do you find your employees? Can they just take everything…?"

What the soldiers didn't know was that I had ensured I had full access. It looked as if I were the employee assigned to manage the grocery store because I had made IDs for myself and others and had predated everything.

Prior to the invasion, it was all about following the rules in Kuwait. Refugees like my family had to follow the rules to maintain their status. When the war hit, I threw the rules out the proverbial window. Not only did I need to survive, but I was also responsible for keeping my community fed. Call it survival mode or intuition, but those were the steps I chose.

I hired people and ensured they showed up on time; I scheduled their work hours, delivered groceries, and portioned food for Iraqi soldiers and Kuwaiti citizens. I soon figured out how to appease soldiers who wanted to clear out my inventory. A little negotiation kept them happy—and kept me safe.

I also learned how to manage the panicked families who wanted to hoard food. I mapped out the city into blocks so that

I could drop off basic grocery items for them. I even learned how to drive at night during curfew to deliver groceries to customers who would otherwise starve if I didn't reach them. I navigated military checkpoints, fired employees, and haggled with suppliers.

I also learned to be wary and how to discipline my words and activities when interacting with suppliers. I couldn't risk them tipping off the Iraqi soldiers about me—or demanding money for their silence.

Every day I collected cash. However, I couldn't risk being discovered with a large amount of money, as the soldiers could easily kill me, grab the cash, and jeopardize the food supply. Fortunately, many of the Iraqi soldiers I interacted with were kind: they cared what happened to me and didn't want me hurt!

But most of all, during those tense days and nights, I struggled to say as little as possible to my parents about the dangers I faced: I didn't want them to worry.

When I reflect on those perilous times, I realize it was a miracle that I didn't lose my life—and indeed that it was miraculous that I also gained unforgettable entrepreneurship lessons for free! However, nothing is free. The experience did cost me: I had to leave my family in Kuwait and my college plans imploded because of Iraq's invasion. Eventually, I reached the United States—instead of Canada—in the fall of

1990 on Halloween night. I began my first business: selling T-shirts. Soon afterwards, I was selling perfumes.

If you had told me back then that I was an entrepreneur, I would have asked, “What do you mean?” In fact, I may still ask that now (smile)! All I know is that one must plan, learn, and evolve as an entrepreneur. A backup plan is also helpful. Life, as I learned that August day in Kuwait, is always changing.

Now you may well ask, “Faris, how does any of this relate to 7-7-7 Marketing?” Well, you’ll discover that I learned a great many lessons from my reflections on what I experienced and what worked or didn’t work. I sincerely hope that this glimpse into the background to the 7-7-7 Marketing strategy motivates you to try a few new things in your own business.

"In those early days, if someone told me NO, I became upset. Over the years, I've learned to celebrate when someone says NO — because that got me closer to my next YES!" — Faris Alami on "Celebrate the 'No'"

CHAPTER 1
WHAT IS MARKETING?

When I arrived in Tucson, Arizona in 1990, I was desperate to work but unable to land a job. Although I tried, potential employers rejected me several times. My limited English and my few resources compelled me to try new things to earn money. Hunger was my drive to survive.

I had a six-month student visa and slept on friends' couches or at the mosque, where I spent several nights. Everyone there was so helpful. Mohammed, the mosque guardian, allowed me to sleep in the guest room when it was unoccupied. Being by myself in a quiet, enormous building was scary, but I appreciated the shelter. I could have been sleeping on the sidewalk.

The room was warm and safe. There was no refrigerator or kitchen—just a sleeping room—and I was grateful. The room's gray walls and white ceilings comforted me. I wasn't at someone's house; I was hosted in God's house, and God was good to me.

Life was far from secure, however. I needed an income and a consistent one. I designed T-shirts for the mosque to support them in raising funds for humanitarian causes. This led to my full-fledged T-shirt business. I learned later how to sell new products and perfumes. At first, it seemed to take forever to succeed; I couldn't even make a single twenty-five-dollar sale. During my first three days as a business owner, my total sales amounted to—zero.

Eventually, however, my T-shirt business allowed me to move into an apartment, and although my income never surpassed two hundred or four hundred dollars per month, I was grateful. The money provided a roof over my head and at least one large meal a day.

With disappointment and need burning a hole in my stomach, I adapted quickly and changed my approach. I didn't have the luxury of waiting. I was desperate, so I had to act. I shifted my sales methods. Along with the lessons had learned at the Kuwaiti grocery store, I relied on keen observation and incorporated some helpful strategies. It may have taken me a while, but in due course I figured it out, thanks to the insights gained from my work and what I had learned from others.

Marketing and sales

Before proceeding, let me begin by defining marketing. When first starting out as an entrepreneur, you might confuse marketing and sales. The goal of making money may obscure how an entrepreneur actually does so. While you'll find a formal definition in the dictionary, I define marketing as all the activities you undertake to generate an awareness of your product and services. It's the look-at-what-I-offer flag that entrepreneurs often wave at potential customers. Those "flags" can be flyers, brochures, and advertisements. Marketing happens before you sell anything.

On the other hand, a sale is the actual transaction that results when a customer signs on the dotted line or clicks "buy now" on a website or mobile app. Selling is asking a customer to decide about what you've marketed to them and to take an action to buy.

Let me add one more definition. Branding is a separate concept from marketing. Branding is how people perceive your products and services. Customers define the experience your product gives them and that product's value to them. As entrepreneurs, we may pursue elaborate branding activities, but ultimately, customers frame your brand. They determine who you are in the marketplace.

The numbers game

Marketing and sales were new concepts to me when I first started in the business. What I learned through observation was simple: marketing is a numbers game. The more people I reached through marketing, the more interactions I converted to tangible sales.

Initially, I spoke with roughly twenty people a day. Every person said "no." My lack of results crushed me. Hadn't I spoken to hundreds of people? No. In fact, once I counted my interactions, I found I had only spoken to ten people. *Ten.* No wonder I wasn't seeing results. My sales efforts fell below those of my peers working around me simply because they spoke to significantly more people.

Understanding my lead conversion rate

Unknown to me, my disappointing sales were, in fact, providing information about my lead conversion rate. I was learning, in real time, my effectiveness in converting the people I spoke with into customers. I began to understand that I needed to interact with one hundred people to create at least ten sales. There are countless articles, books, and studies, both medical and non-medical, showing that for every one hundred touches, perhaps ten people will buy. Mike, another salesperson I knew, told me that. There is an array of software—from Google Analytics to ads to many other CRM

(Customer Relationship Manager) tools—that will help you understand lead conversion and can support such activities and matrix creations.

After taking the time to reflect on my initial mediocre performance, it appears that, while my first business venture was rudimentary, I've applied the same lead conversion process to every venture since then. *Intentionally and frequently interacting* with potential customers has been my guiding principle throughout my business career.

The marketing principles remain the same

Starting a business can be challenging, exciting, and daunting all at once. From building and growing businesses to being a strategic partner with government and business leaders in over one hundred countries, I've observed that marketing's foundational principles remain the same: everything begins with relationships. These relationships can stem from the buyer, based on his or her needs or wants, the product connections, the brand connection, or the seller. Let me explain. Your friend Khaled asks you to get product ABC. You'll obtain that product based on your relationship with him and his relationship with the product, the brand, or the person or shop selling it. It's all about relationships!

Grasping this concept will distinguish you from other entrepreneurs. According to the U.S. Census Bureau, aspiring entrepreneurs registered 4.3. million new businesses in the United States during 2021.[1] This was a 24 percent increase above the previous year. In the first part of 2022, the number of registered businesses was still rising, according to the Census Bureau's Business Formation Statistics.[2] However, as of this writing, with worries about inflation and with a recession on the horizon, the number of registered businesses was down 2.6 percent in June compared with May.[3]

As fewer entrepreneurs jump into the arena and customers watch their dollars, insightful and effective marketing will be paramount. Simply offering a marketable product or service won't be enough. Knowing how to market to customers is the key to growth and success.

From the days of my T-shirt marketing and sales efforts to my perfume business—which eventually operated in seven U.S. states—to the days when I worked with Macy's, Bath & Body Works, and other companies, to my current activities in executive management at International Strategic Management, I've learned to understand that nurturing relationships is the foundation of effective marketing.

Marketing is the stepping-stone to generating sales.

Marketing is the stepping-stone to generating sales. And to gain sales, you must reach people. At first, you cast a wide net. With time and effort, you will identify your ideal customer. As mentioned earlier, I discovered that the more people I interacted with, the more people I identified who wanted to buy or needed to buy, and the faster I completed sales.

The profile of my ideal customer took shape the more I reached out to people and refined my marketing outreaches. Having an ideal customer does not mean all customers are not welcome. All are welcome, of course, but I encourage you to focus on the ideal customer to experience a greater return.

Customize your marketing style

Individuals have their own unique sales style. I learned this by working with Sam. Sam loved selling inside office buildings—and he was amazing. He could perform ten to twenty transactions in a single day. When I worked in office buildings, however, I sold nothing.

While I canvassed urban areas, Sam preferred the suburbs. What was our common denominator? We both spoke to at least one hundred people per day. That's what connected us—not our sales styles or location preferences. For entrepreneurs just starting out, take heed: what works for you may not work for someone else. There are plenty of marketing and sales templates out there, so take the time to weigh them against your strengths, weaknesses, preferences, and business circumstances.

This book is a place to chat

While you may want to deploy this strategy, it's not meant to be the only one: it's designed to be part of overall strategies and tactics you can use. And please don't view it as "Faris is right and I'm wrong!" It's meant to be a conversation starter about what you're doing to attract and retain customers.

Let me mention this before you read on. At the beginning of every chapter, I've included excerpts from my blog posts on entrepreneurship and also refer to my blogs posts often in this book as reference points. In addition, I've added an "Action" step and I conclude my chapters with a section called "A Finjan Moment." "Action" requires no explanation but "A Finjan Moment" does.

Finjan is Arabic for a small cup of coffee or tea. I host "The Finjan Show" podcast, which features an honest conversation with everyday entrepreneurs. Like my podcast, "A Finjan Moment" offers business tips as if we were chatting face to face.

I hope you enjoy it.

A FINJAN MOMENT

Just because you are doing marketing, don't assume sales will come along. Marketing and sales represent two different cycles.

ACTION

Take time to assess your marketing approach. Review what you've learned and identify areas where you want to improve in your marketing.

"One of the most powerful ways to stay relevant in a crowded business world is to provide consistent messaging with gentle reminders that you are here to serve your customer/client needs or desires." — Faris Alami on "The Power of 7-7-7 Marketing"

CHAPTER 2
THE POWER OF SEVEN

Marketing is more than a catchy phrase. It isn't passive or random: it's intentional and meaningful. Thinking about marketing that way, however, may make it seem overwhelming or too difficult to achieve. Many people don't pursue marketing because it seems like an unattainable goal. You want to become more profitable, but just talking about marketing your business seems far off. It's like the prize you long for but don't know how to reach.

I fully understand if this is how you feel at the moment as we begin to dig deeper into 7-7-7 Marketing. The steps I offer are an organic way to build your business—layer upon layer. All I ask is that while reading these pages, you make a commitment to yourself to complete the book at your own pace. There is truth to the old saying that Rome wasn't built in a day. Building your business will take time too.

I also ask that you be purposeful as you try out the practices outlined in this book. Assess how they fit with what you're already accomplishing in your business. If a step works, add it to your marketing plan. If it doesn't fit your business right now, try it later on. My goal is to help facilitate your success by providing you with effective tools, not to browbeat you into a specific way of doing things.

Moreover, after working with thousands of entrepreneurs, I also understand that everyone learns at various levels and speeds. They also obtain information for different needs. One of you may grasp one part of 7-7-7 Marketing right away, while someone else may need to pause there for a minute. Learning a new system and integrating it within your existing marketing efforts can be demanding. Allow me to encourage you: follow the action steps, assess what can work for your business—and breathe. You got this!

The path to results

I hope you understand that in order to see results, you must follow the exact steps in the 7-7-7 Marketing approach and be willing to adapt and change. Adopting the 7-7-7 Marketing approach is a process: it will take time to take root and you'll have to repeat it as well.

I can't guarantee anything: your results will be yours alone. However, I stand by the powerful results I've achieved so far and have seen others achieve. Please forgive the self-promotion, but while you can do this alone, International Strategic Management (ISM) would be honored to help you integrate 7-7-7 Marketing into your business.

Two more thoughts before we begin in earnest. First, the marketing strategy I present here isn't the only one around. The marketing resources available to entrepreneurs across all platforms are vast! But I do hope you'll include the 7-7-7 Marketing strategy in your portfolio of marketing approaches, and that after implementing the steps, you'll let me know what worked and what didn't.

Second, the 7-7-7 Marketing strategy is not a substitute for your bread-and-butter business activities. While you consider this strategy, operate your business as you usually do and keep providing exceptional customer service. Take the time to decide whether you want to integrate 7-7-7 Marketing into your current marketing activities.

Now let's get started.

Early in my sales career, I observed—and learned—that most of the time, people buy as a result of the different "sales touches" they might have with you. "Touches" are the ways potential customers engage with you or with your products and services.

> A marketing framework that attracts clients and builds meaningful relationships is the fuel that empowers businesses to prosper.

Studies have shown that sometimes people don't buy until the tenth sales touch.[1] Entrepreneurs who understand this cycle of touches *plan* their interactions with customers.[2] Behind each outreach, sales pitch or marketing campaign are insights drawn from the multiple sales touches customers usually require before they decide to buy.

Which brings me back to 7-7-7 Marketing. As I mentioned earlier, my marketing strategy addresses the multiple touches required to achieve a sale. The strategy is very relational. A marketing framework that attracts clients and builds meaningful relationships is the fuel that empowers businesses to prosper. My system calculates seven touches instead of ten, and it's intended to get you started in a highly relational form of marketing. Think 7-7-7. The three sevens stand for three steps:

People: seven people you want to contact within organizations or companies.

Marketing methods: seven ways you can reach out to a potential customer.

Marketing timeline: seven days, weeks, months—how long it takes you to contact the customer.

How do you apply these three sevens to your business? Suppose that today you get a postcard from your local dealership about the latest model of your favorite car. You may not buy immediately, but you make mental notes. *Wow. I like that*, you think.

A few days later, you hear about that car again from a friend. And soon afterward, you see a YouTube video demonstrating the car's new features.

The following month, you're in a meeting and someone mentions the car. A few months later, en route to the airport, you glimpse a billboard advertising the car.

During the conference you're attending, volunteers distribute a flyer about the new model. The carmaker is a sponsor. On the flight home, you thumb through an airline magazine: a sleek ad features the new model. You smile.

Through multiple touches, the carmaker has managed to reach you—and not necessarily only through marketing from one specific dealership.

Similarly, I want you to understand marketing strategies and their required actions. If you study marketing campaigns, you may also notice how they target customers like you using specific images and content. Everything is geared so that the marketer can attract the ideal customers the business seeks.

It really helps if you have some understanding of who your customers are or could be. (Your ideal customer may change, so you can always adjust.) You also need to know what they want and what they expect from your products and services. Once you've done this, you're climbing the Mount Everest of business! Of course, you'll never know *completely* what drives your ideal customer to buy, but the idea is to know something about them and keep on studying what they like and need. The more knowledge you have about your ideal customer, the higher you'll get on that mountain!

And as you climb higher and higher in business, you can plan your interactions with existing customers and prospects. 7-7-7 Marketing gives you a blueprint that enables you to interact with your customers in terms of your contact with them over time.

How to do it

In my blog post "7-7-7 Marketing" I outline how to create a list of three types of prospective or optional customers and clients.[3] First, you have "Should Be" customers. Second are the "Need to Be" customers. Third are the "Dream" customers.

The “Should Be” list will include seven customers you may have lost, or who were once your clients, or who have been talking to you for a while. Reviewing past projects or sales you’ve achieved will identify customers you can reconnect with and learn what their needs are. Their responses may surprise you. Even before you reached out to them, they may have been thinking about you and the services you provide.

The “Need to Be” list includes those customers you should help because you serve others like them. For example, if you work with one doctor’s office, assume other doctors may hire you because they require your services. Consider other doctors’ offices with a minimum of two locations. Aim for five locations as the ideal. Collect seven names of doctors’ offices and you have your customer list. Don’t be shy! You have a reason to reach out because you’ve already served doctors. This list should be easy to create. You’ve already worked in this niche and may discover many opportunities right under your eyes—if you only look.

The “Dream” list includes customers you wish would buy your products or services. A good example is a large institution such as a hospital—a major organization you would like the privilege of serving. Really think about who you would serve if you could. The dream client could be global business owners, celebrities, pivotal community leaders, cool startups, religious congregations, entire neighborhoods, states—even nations. Dream big!

STEP 1	Create your lists
STEP 2	Schedule your contact dates
STEP 3	Choose your contact methods

Once you've compiled your three lists, you're ready to apply the 7-7-7 Marketing process. Suppose the ABC tech startup on your "Should Be" list is an ideal customer for your product or service.

These suggestions are aimed at *one* potential customer on a single list. Repeat these steps with six other potential customers. Once you finish your lists, sit back and see what you've accomplished. You've come up with seven sets of names for the "Should Be," "Need to Be," and "Dream" lists you've created.

I hope you can feel your optimism growing. Did creating these lists stimulate your creativity? I hope so, because as you work with the 7-7-7 Marketing process, your lists are never skimpy. Take the time to celebrate that! You have at least twenty-one potential customers or clients to reach out to during the next seven days, weeks, or months.

Choose your contact method

Now that you have your list of customers, the second step is to engage them in ways that matter. Using the 7-7-7

Marketing process, take some time to think of seven ways to reach out to them. In fact, take a lot of time. Be imaginative. Think about what that ideal customer would like to receive from your business.

You can email them in one week, send them something by mail the following week, call them the third week, seek them out at an event the fourth week, and so on. Or it can be as simple as sending them weekly emails for seven weeks straight. Here's an example of planned interactions with a customer:

- At first, you could call and introduce yourself and leave your card. In a month, you could stop by with a small gift basket that includes a special message. In the third month, you could say congrats when their child graduates or a local article features the owner.

- In the fourth month, you could reach out to them via your newsletter. During the fifth month, you could draw their attention to a conference they might find interesting, or mention where you're speaking or hosting a booth.

- In the sixth month, you could mention your new blog, which touches on a subject they care about. During the seventh month, you stop by and ask about when you could do business together.

The tone of each interaction with customers should be cordial. Avoid pushy text or careless words: it's a soft-shoe dance. To continue the metaphor, let them know you're willing to partner with them—but don't drag them across the dance floor! Meet them where they are. And be considerate about how often you contact them. Will it be weekly, monthly, quarterly, yearly? Discern what fits them best. Each business is different.

Schedule your contact dates

The third step in 7-7-7 Marketing is to reach out to the people on your newly minted lists over the time period you choose. I've shown you how to do that in the earlier example about planned interactions. But let me emphasize here that your tools will be critical: you need to track your progress.

Whether you're working through Google, Outlook, Calendly, or any other appointment-setting tool, master your calendar. You could also use Excel sheets to track your customer list and record when you reach out to them—and of course you can use your CRM system.

The point is, schedule your contact dates. Whether you choose seven weeks, seven months, or seven days, your contacts must be documented: you've got to see what's working.

When you finish the entire process, you could have up to ten names on each list. But keep in mind: how much can you really do in addition to everything you have to beyond this activity?

Facing obstacles

Let's say you reach a decision-maker on your list and they decline to do business with you. Obviously, you don't want to reach out to them in that campaign, so remove their name from your list. However, make a note to contact them annually or perhaps in a few years if anything changes.

Once you've finished the first round of 7-7-7, swap out their name on your working seven-client list, add another name, and continue following the 7-7-7 Marketing steps I've mentioned:

People: seven people you want to contact within organizations or companies.

Marketing methods: seven ways you can reach out to a potential customer.

Marketing timeline: seven days, weeks, months—how long it takes you to contact the customer.

The success of seven

While nothing is perfect, this process works best when you keep it going while carrying on other activities. It will not work on its own! At ISM, we've been blessed to work with many businesses and have seen their success once they've incorporated 7-7-7 Marketing into their processes.

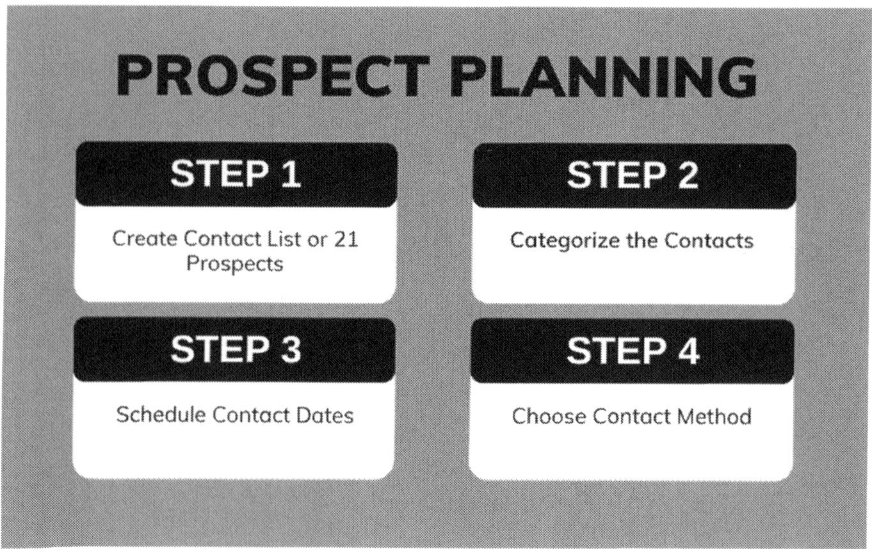

I offer 7-7-7 Marketing as one marketing approach. There are many others. Think back on the successful sales conversions you've experienced, either recently or over the years. What key steps led to those sales conversions? What were the outcomes? Identify what worked and what failed. Remember: people do business with people. They do business with people who practice professionalism and integrity. With people who show up when they're needed. Strive to be that person.

A FINJAN MOMENT

Remember to recycle the twenty-one names. After reaching the initial seven contacts, move them to once a month, or quarterly. You might also move some to a list for a yearly contact, depending on what happens with that contact. After you recycle the names, refresh the lists with seven new people in each category.

ACTION

Think about your customers and prospects. How can you help them? How should you interact with them?

"Despite the ubiquity of technology and social media, building a network happens in person, face to face, in rooms, around tables, over coffee. Building a network requires building relationships, and building relationships requires connection and vulnerability. New or young entrepreneurs may not fully grasp this." — Faris Alami on Strength in Numbers"

CHAPTER 3
REACHING PEOPLE

People-centric marketing converts to sales. You may hear differently elsewhere, but I encourage you to focus on people. Even if you automate your marketing, optimize your website, and produce award-winning podcasts, focus your marketing on the solution, meaning the benefits of your service or product, rather than the features.

Aim for a shoe-leather approach. Get to the people. Connect with them. If you skip people, expect little success with your business. For example, think of how flashy marketing may have drawn you to a new establishment; but when the establishment didn't focus on your needs, did you want to go back?

Whatever you do, work hard not to jeopardize your relationships with the customers you serve. Relationship building is a basic form of marketing. I encourage every entrepreneur to consider investing time in building relationships or at least connecting with people who can bring you business through *their* relationships.

If relationships aren't your forte, start networking with other entrepreneurs to gain some practice time. As you meet business peers, gaining insights from them and sharing your own observations, you'll pick up the art of relating to people. Networking gets easier with practice. I promise.

> People-centric marketing converts to sales.

Please remember to give yourself a break. Everyone has different styles, and it takes time to effortlessly navigate a room with distinct personalities, interests, and cultures. Once you get the hang of it, I hope you find meeting people as rewarding as I do. Every in-person meeting is a chance to explore the world around us.

If you can attend a chamber meeting or an industry event in person, do so. Chat with people. Be interested in what they say. Simply going on and on about who you are and what you do isn't going to gain you new friends. On the contrary: it alienates people. At the end of a conversation, ask for someone's card and note how you met them in your contact list. Remember at least one thing about them. The checklist below may help get you started. It's a recap of what I discuss in "The Finjan Show: The Art of Networking Part I" and in "The Finjan Show: The Art of Networking Part II." [1, 2]

1. **Arrive early.** Shoot for fifteen or five minutes early, depending on the event and platform. This is a great way to observe and meet people before things get underway.

2. **Start a conversation.** You're building a relationship.

3. **Don't just talk about yourself.** Be interested. Ask questions. Get people engaged and make them feel comfortable talking about themselves.

4. **Be interested in their answers.** Absorb what they're saying and follow up with questions. Allow time for them to ask *you* questions or change the subject.

5. **Resist treating networking as a sale-a-thon.** Discern whether an aggressive sales posture is appropriate for the networking setting.

6. **Facilitate friendships.** Introduce contacts to other people. Be helpful.

7. **Avoid dropping names.** Mention names only when it's purposeful. If you can help someone with a name, if there's a specific reason to do so, and if it's appropriate in that networking setting, then by all means go ahead.

8. **Ask for their card.** Now you have the opportunity to follow up with them. They may ask you to contact them on LinkedIn, Instagram, etc. They may also ask for your card!

9. **Follow up.** It may seem old-fashioned, but I've found that people are very appreciative when I mail cards. Texts and Facebook Messenger also work and offer an alternative to email.

10. **Don't let the past affect your networking.** One previous unpleasant networking experience doesn't necessarily mean it will happen again. Consider networking opportunities as a step toward a fresh start.

Networking can happen anywhere

You may think business is about selling or promoting. I'm here to tell you that building a business—and this is from someone who came to the United States as an immigrant and began with nothing—starts with relationships. My first delivery of good business generated more business.

You may also think that networking only happens during an industry event or mixer. Not so. Networking can happen anywhere—from elevators to parks. By interacting with people, you establish a relationship with someone who could end up being your friend, not just your customer, partner, or supplier. Networking ignites human connections.

Marketing and networking are business cousins. Both of them thrive when you focus on the customer. Throughout this book, you'll learn the basics of both those skills.

A FINJAN MOMENT

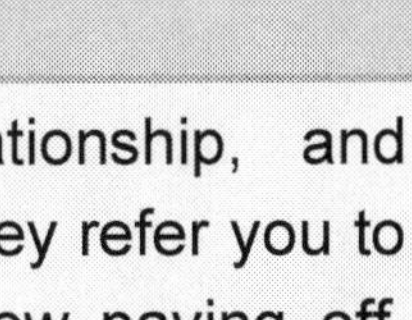

If you're strategically building a relationship, and someone gets to know you better, and they refer you to someone, your networking efforts are now paying off. You're working within their network, and that's a huge step.

ACTION

How can you increase your networking activities? How can you refine them?

“Stop doubting and start questioning. It will allow you to think about answers and solutions, whereas doubting will only leave you sitting there, feeling unable to do anything.” — Faris Alami on “Never Doubt, Always Question”

CHAPTER 4
PLAN YOUR BUSINESS

There are two kinds of business plans: a formal plan used for seeking funding or partnerships, and an informal one we call a "napkin" plan, which entrepreneurs use to keep on track during the preliminary stages of a new business, product, or idea.

Entrepreneurs use the formal business plan for funding or other needs, typically when communicating with external stakeholders. Creating this plan takes time and lots of research, but once you're finished, you'll have a broad view of what you can accomplish as an entrepreneur.

Traditional business plans take longer to research, write, and assemble, according to the Small Business Association (SBA). These plans are detailed and typically include an executive summary, company description, market analysis, a description of your company's organization and management, details about your service or product line, marketing and sales, your specific funding request, what you expect your financial projections to be, and an appendix.[1]

The "napkin plan" or, as the SBA calls it, the "lean startup" is faster to write.[2] In it you will outline business partnerships and activities, such as leveraging technology or some sort of business advantage. Then you will identify resources that make you stand out among competitors, such as a diverse staff or a unique intellectual property.

The business plan must explain your value proposition. If you're in the vegan food delivery business, for example, how do you differ from other vegan delivery services? Is it your menu, your packaging, or your promised delivery time? Your value proposition will include these details.

You will also describe your ideal customer and outline their customer journey when using your product or service. What are the demographics for your ideal customer? Does the customer use a mobile app or simply walk into your store?

Your plan must identify what channels you'll use to reach customers.

Your napkin/lean startup business plan

Lastly, your napkin/lean startup business plan will explain how you intend to make money. You'll describe the costs you'll incur, how you'll manage them, and how profits will be generated through one or more revenue streams.

In our experience, most entrepreneurs begin with a napkin/lean startup plan. It's a more immediate step and one that's necessary, given to time, resources, and circumstances. Entrepreneurs who choose this route have typically outlined their business basics as follows:

Napkin/Lean Startup Plan
• How much money can I make on this opportunity?
• How much do I need to sell to make a profit?
• How long will it take me to break even and go beyond?
• What tools do I need to immediately start work?
• Will I need to buy leads?

Whichever business plan you choose, take time to quiz yourself. Set aside some quiet time to get a broad perspective of what your business will achieve. I encourage you not to skip this step. Being aware of your goals and what's required to reach them will speed up your success as an entrepreneur. When you're ready, go to Chapter Twelve and answer additional questions and take notes.

Questions
• What is your product?
• Who is your ideal customer?
• What are your customer segments?
• Who will be your management team?
• Do you require marketing? What about market research and collateral materials?
• What is your primary, secondary and even third market?
• What are your estimated profits over a three- to five-year period?
• Will you be able to support the business 100 percent through sales?
• Will you need outside funding? If so, how much?
• Do you need office space? Will you lease or buy? Will you purchase furniture? Can you share a co-working space?
• Will your business be retail or manufacturing?

• What equipment and supplies do you need?
• What will be your communications and utilities costs?
• What licenses and permits are required?
• What are your insurance costs?
• Have you retained an attorney and an accountant?
• Will you have inventory to store? Are there associated costs?
• What will you pay employees?

The SBA provides additional guidance and business plan samples.[3] You can use templates or you can assemble a business plan from scratch. At International Strategic Management (ISM), we have our own templates that we use when working with clients and partners. The SBA also provides information on these planning steps:

Planning steps
• Market research and competitive analysis
• Write your business plan
• Calculate your startup costs
• Establish business credit

• Fund your business
• Buy an existing business or franchise

What is your MVP?

You've heard of the "Most Valuable Player" in a sports context, but MVP in business means "Minimum Viable Product." This term defines the most basic product version you can launch. Getting a basic product out there—at a low cost—can provide you with feedback from customers about whether your product provides value.

The knowledge you gain can determine how you develop your product. A good idea becomes a great idea after you put it to the test. Think hard about your MVP. According to Forbes magazine, firms such as Dropbox, Slack, and even Uber got their start using MVPs.[4]

Allow me to add an important caveat. You don't have to wait until things are perfect to launch. Perfectionism can delay success. You can discover solutions if you keep moving. Isn't that what inflation, talent shortages, and the pandemic have taught us after years of Zoom meetings and phone calls? I know it's difficult, considering everything going on around us, but shake off the doubts holding you back. As much as you're able to, strive for solid solutions and for answers to your business challenges. I also urge you to set realistic goals.

Entrepreneurs are often distracted in the moment, but goals keep you aligned on your entrepreneurial journey. As I wrote on Medium in the blog post "Setting Long-Term Goals," you can "call them SMART goals: Simple, Measurable, Achievable, Relevant, and Time-bound. No matter what you call them, the key is to be clear about what the goals entail."[5]

When working with entrepreneurs and leaders around the world, I've often noticed that people in under-served, under-represented, and under-resourced communities often wrestle with doubts about their performance as entrepreneurs. They often believe they aren't skilled enough or simply "not worth it." When I hear this train of thought during my coaching, I immediately challenge it! Looking at what your business concept lacks and staying stuck in that place won't open any doors for you. Doubting yourself as an entrepreneur never carries you forward. Never. So, *always question, but never doubt!*

> You don't have to wait until things are perfect to launch.

Instead, I urge entrepreneurs and leaders to take stock of the resources they have and to own that. By leveraging what you manage and what you can create, you open yourself to realizing that what you own has value. You're assessing what *you own* and brainstorming *your way* to solutions and answers.

Questions	
What do I have that I can start with?	What do I need to complete the activity or project?
What do I have to start at least now?	Can I do it any other way?
What can I do to shift my mindset?	What questions can I ask myself to help me move forward?
What tools have I utilized in the past to stop doubting and start questioning?	What have I overcome in the past?

Always know there is help if you want it. There are successful business owners around you who would be glad to mentor entrepreneurs. At ISM, we love to coach. We offer planning help for marketing, sales, and operations, and we'll show you how to advance from a startup to become a flourishing enterprise with sustainable growth.

We also advise entrepreneurs on identifying their market and selecting the best technologies to advance their business. ISM also advises entrepreneurs on diversifying a business, such as going from residential to commercial real estate or expanding a business to other countries. Over the years, my

ISM team has learned how to support businesses in a variety of industries, stages, backgrounds, and ecosystems from next-to-nothing to fully-run enterprises. I am thankful for all these amazing opportunities, which have allowed me to enjoy experiences that I can now share with you!

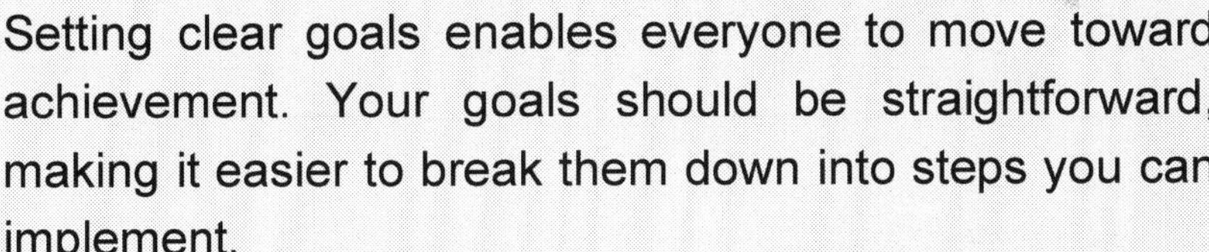

Setting clear goals enables everyone to move toward achievement. Your goals should be straightforward, making it easier to break them down into steps you can implement.

ACTION

Compile notes on planning your business. Assess how you want to shape your products and services for the long term.

"There are six life cycles that every Entrepreneur must know by heart in order to grow their business." — Faris Alami on "The Life Cycle of a Customer"

CHAPTER 5
THE LIFE CYCLE OF A BUSINESS

Every entrepreneur wants to reach customers and, as much as possible, provide them with the products and services they need. Entrepreneurs dream of a successful marketing campaign that leads to months of customer queries, endless referrals from satisfied clients, and a sales funnel stuffed with orders.

Those dreams can turn into nightmares, however, when entrepreneurs neglect to understand the six life cycles of a business. They may know the cycles but have never thought of them in this context. I promise you that knowing these cycles will help sustain long-term growth for your business. When challenges arise, you can use the life cycle of a business and search for clues that may show you what to improve or what to stop doing. The six life cycles provide a glimpse into why your business is successful. I've discussed these cycles in "The Life Cycle of a Customer":[1]

The Life Cycle of Attraction: When you initially contact a customer, how long does it take for them to say "yes" and buy from you? The time usually ranges from twenty-four hours to nine months for most retail businesses. Three to eighteen months is how long it typically takes for service industries. View this as a courtship between you and a customer. Take a few moments to think about your business. How much time elapses before customers buy?[2]

The Life Cycle of Transaction: Once customers have said "yes" and have decided to buy from you, how long does it take to effect a transaction?[3]

The Life Cycle of Frequency: Sales transactions can occur every day. For some businesses, not so much. Some customers may court a business more infrequently. Think once a month, maybe once a year. How often do customers buy your products and services?[4]

The Life Cycle of Expansion: When a customer reaches out for additional products or services you offer, it's a gift. Have you ever calculated how long it takes before a customer asks you about another product you offer?[5]

The Life Cycle of Referral: Now, here's the gold ring. Referrals widen the reach of your business. Before reading further, think about referrals you've received from clients. What did you do to make them satisfied customer?[6]

The Life Cycle of Growth: It's hard to imagine, but the courtship dance between you and a customer can cease—and not necessarily for negative reasons. Customers may outgrow what a business offers or no longer need its products and services. Sometimes the business outgrows its initial customer base. Whatever the cause, entrepreneurs need to calculate how many transactions must take place before the courtship ends.[7]

When a customer reaches out for additional products or services you offer, it's a gift. The six life cycles of business allow you to plan realistic business targets and goals more effectively. They equip you to observe the current state of your business with deeper insight, assess its viability, plot future performance, and pivot to business strengths whenever necessary.

When a customer reaches out for additional products or services you offer, it's a gift.

Every entrepreneur should know the six life cycles. When you can't assess your sales cycle comprehensively, you hinder potential success. We'll give you more time to think about the life cycle of a business in Chapter Twelve.

Before we go on and discuss the sales process itself, however, I want to take a moment to address your mindset as entrepreneur. Please stay with me. How you frame your business activities will impact your success. As I wrote in "The Entrepreneurial Mindset," being an entrepreneur is *a way of thinking*:[8]

"Aspiring entrepreneurs may have a different view than those that have been around a while. In a small or mid-size business, those who did not personally start the company might hold a different perspective than those who did."

"Sometimes, we have to re-frame how we receive or interpret what we see or hear. No matter where you are in the world, a single word or phrase can have very different meaning[s]. The real key is how entrepreneurs react to what they see in the marketplace. We all believe, at a high level, that entrepreneurs are individuals that see an opportunity in the marketplace or a problem they would like to solve, or an opportunity to provide some type of service or product to the marketplace.

"Some do deep investigations and others just jump right in. Either way, at a high level, that is what we believe entrepreneurs do. Some say they are risk-takers. The bottom line is this: understanding the mindset of how an entrepreneur works can help aspiring entrepreneurs to act."[9]

How you see yourself, your business, and your business environment will determine the trajectory of your success. If you don't believe you can implement your business goals despite the odds, you've determined the boundaries for your enterprise. No one else does.

That zoning law, tax district, food safety inspector or funding issue didn't permanently slow or stop your business. Your thinking did! Whenever an entrepreneur clings to a specific point of view, *it* becomes their reality, not the obstacles they face. If you assume a certain business environment is too difficult for you and refuse to do your due diligence and get coaching, then yes, that environment is too tough to run your business. If fear underlies your business pursuits, those pernicious doubts become reality.

I urge you as an aspiring entrepreneur or as a veteran business owner to view yourself and the world around you positively and to expect to soar high. This does not mean that you can't be realistic about your circumstances; I only ask that you look at what you have accomplished and not let others determine what success means to you.

LIFE CYCLE BUSINESS QUESTIONS

Assessing your business profile

HOW STRONG IS YOUR BUSINESS STORY?

How long does it take for the customer to come by after they view your website or ad? Days, months, years? Does your public display of products and services compel them to learn more?

WHAT IS THEIR JOURNEY WITH YOU AS A CUSTOMER?

How long does it take to buy from you? After initial conversations and proposals do they jump at the chance to work with you? Is their journey easy or difficult?

HOW LONG DO THEY STAY WITH YOU?

Do they come back every week? Once a year, every four years? Is your website so sticky that they keep searching for your specials? Do you have a newsletter that draws them?

DO CUSTOMERS BRAG ON YOU?

How long before they promote you to their friends? Have you measured how much of your business is word-of-mouth?

DO THEY CRAVE NEW PRODUCTS & SERVICES?

How long before they buy additional services or products from you? Are they compelled to buy new products and services from you because they love how you do business?

A FINJAN MOMENT 

While a customer may buy from you as often as you think appropriate, there may come a time where they simply stop purchasing from your company. There's an average of how long a customer stays with you, and you should know what that time frame is.

ACTION

Assess the six cycles of a business as they apply to your company. How does it affect your goal setting?

"Make sure you implement little processes or steps that make your products or services different from the rest." — Faris Alami on "Sweat the Small Stuff"

CHAPTER 6
THE SALES CYCLE PROCESS

Do you know how long it takes for your customer to complete a transaction with your business? Each step matters in your sales cycle process, and to develop a sustainable business, you need to know those steps inside and out. When you track your steps toward a sale, you gain clues about what works and what doesn't.

For example, do you check whether your e-commerce website runs optimally? Is your site easy to navigate? Slow loading pages or a confusing checkout process annoys customers, and you may not get a second chance to reach them.

> When you can't assess your sales cycle comprehensively, you hinder potential success.

When you can't assess your sales cycle comprehensively, you hinder potential success. Have you studied how many steps are required for a customer to complete a transaction with you?

Agreeing on a proposal and negotiating a fee can take days, weeks, or months in some industries. A team may need to be hired, and there may be dependencies on other vendors. Each of these steps is critical to an entrepreneur's sales cycle.

In other business settings, the sales cycle may end after a few minutes at checkout or after a series of clicks on a website with a shopping cart. But how can you shape that sales cycle? What questions should you ask to improve your sales process? Read on.

The sales process

Let's say you sell clothing. Outline the steps it takes to close a sale in a brick-and-mortar retail setting versus online. Many questions used to assess a sales process at a clothing store can apply to an array of products and services. In the action steps at the end of the chapter, you can add questions that fit your sales cycle process.

In-person: A potential customer looks at the clothing; they may try on items and check prices before deciding. They may either purchase or just leave. You can ask yourself the following questions about your business:

In-Store Display
• What's the estimated time it takes for a customer to browse through items in your store?
• Are all store items clearly marked for size and price?
• What's signage like in the store? Does your signage make it easier for customers to find what they need?
• Is the clothing attractively displayed? Do you practice any cross-merchandising? For example, is a dress paired with shoes?
• If you have a store window, is the clothing professionally presented?

In-Store Sales
• Are your salespeople immediately available to provide the customer with new sizes?

• How knowledgeable are your salespeople about your clothing?
• Do you offer any in-store tech that helps people explore your clothing and any accessories? For example, could you equip your salespeople with tablets to track inventory?
• Do your salespeople mention any special offers or upcoming sales to customers?
• Is your brick-and-mortar business integrated with your online presence?

Online: The customer browses photos of the clothing you sell; they review sizes, availability, and cost. They finally decide. They either proceed to checkout and complete a purchase or they leave your website or app altogether. You can ask yourself the following questions:

Website Experience
• How long does it take for your website pages to load?
• Can customers find what they need quickly? Are there multiple ways to find what they need?
• Is "Menu" easy to find?
• Is "Search" where visitors can see it?

• Is your "Contact" information clear?
• Is your site encrypted?
• Are your photos high resolution?
• Is the text easy to read and well written?
• Does the site meet accessibility standards for customers with disabilities?
• How would you rate your calls to action on any given page?
• What's your customer support like? Do you provide a customer support number, a knowledge base or FAQ sheet?
• Is your site optimized for SEO?
• Is your site integrated with your brick-and-mortar business?

Closing the Sale

This is the step every entrepreneur wants to reach. But we can't focus on the euphoria of the moment. Study what happens during the process that leads to the sale. Tweak the process so that closing the sale is a consistent and expected outcome.

In-Store
• How long does checkout take?
• Is a salesperson readily available? Is there always a line?
• What is the average number of items purchased?
• Do salespeople ask customers about their experience?
• Is there a digitized survey you send if you capture a customer's email?
• Are you prepared to accept multiple forms of payment?
• Do you track sales per category to track your most popular or most unpopular products?
• What are your best sales days and times?
• Do you follow compliance standards in your record-keeping for in-store data collection? Is your business compliant with PCI security standards?
• Have you researched the community your business serves? Do you know their shopping habits and preferences?

Online: When a customer buys clothing from you, what is their experience like?

Website
• Do you offer a secure payment process? Is your business PCI compliant?
• Is your website CCPA (and GDPR) compliant?
• Is your privacy policy clearly shown for customers to view?
• Is your website mobile-friendly?
• Do you allow guest checkout? Or just registration?
• If you offer registration, do you use a social sign-on to reduce registration time for customers?
• Do you try to capture the customer's email address for future interaction?
• When a customer goes through checkout, is the price (including sales tax, shipping costs, and any other fees) clearly displayed?
• Do you offer multiple payment methods?
• Does your site display well-known security badges and seals prominently?
• Does your site offer a cart that shows their purchase? Do you provide a progress indicator?
• What is the average number of items purchased?

• What are your best sales days and times?
• Once they pay for an order, do you send a thank you email with a special offer on their next purchase?

Upselling and cross-merchandising

In-person: Have you provided opportunities for customers to consider related products and services in your business?

In-Store
• Once at the register, does the salesperson mention that there is a sale on the jacket, not just the pants the customer purchased?
• Does the salesperson mention a discount for referrals or any loyalty programs?
• Does the salesperson mention trunk shows or online events?

Online: Once at the register, do you provide the customer with any additional items they might consider buying? Do you display items other customers have purchased?

Website
• Do you highlight any preferred customer programs or upcoming sales for similar items?
• During the checkout process, does the customer see information about online-purchases only or can they view options to attend in-store events like trunk shows?
• Do you offer a loyalty program online and points?

As you can see, the more detailed understanding you have about your sales cycle and how you leverage upselling and cross-selling, the better your grasp on your business. The sales cycle is a paramount metric. (Again, I encourage you to learn about your customers as much as you can because while the idea of upselling or cross-selling may sound negative, do it only when it makes sense to the customer based on your understanding of their wants and needs. Please don't make their decision for them: let them decide.)

Study the time it takes to go from attracting a potential customer to enjoying the privilege of serving them. Knowing your own sales cycle helps mitigate friction points and manage expectations for both you and your customer.

A FINJAN MOMENT 

Most entrepreneurs know the sales cycle by memory, or by doing. Passing that information along to team members or a new staff person can create challenges. This is sharable information. Embed this knowledge into your onboarding and when coaching the team until it becomes second nature for everyone.

ACTION

List helpful ways you can teach your sales cycle process to team members.

"The only way to grow as an individual, an organization, or a community is by taking time to reflect on what's been done. This is why I say: do to move forward, reflect to grow." — Faris Alami on "DO to Move Forward/REFLECT to Grow"

CHAPTER 7
PROVIDING PRODUCTS

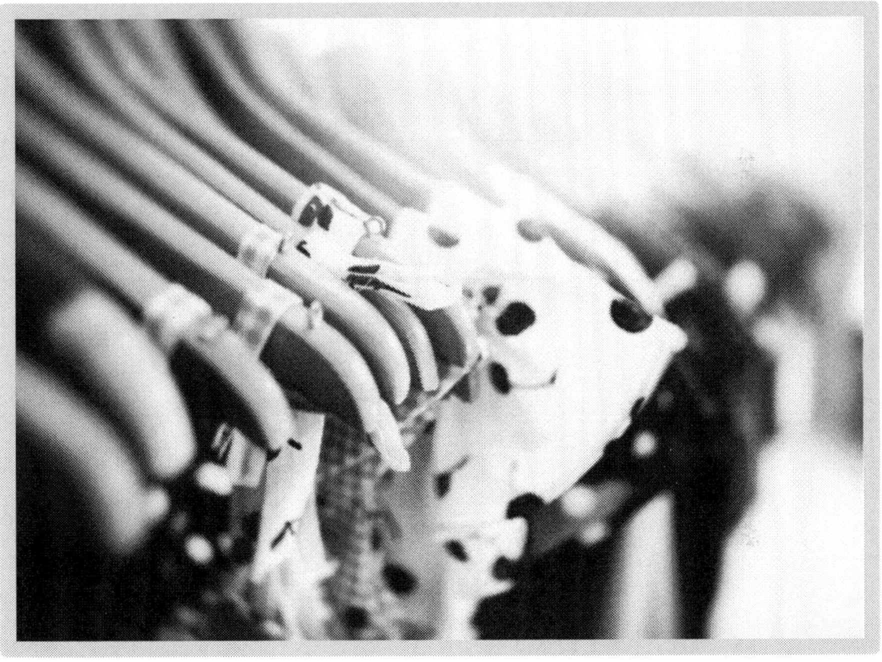

Remember, marketing spreads awareness about your brand, and how people might remember you. Marketing includes your website, flyers, brochures, Instagram and Facebook ads, truck signage, highway billboards, and more. Just because you market a product, never assume sales will necessarily follow.

To explain what I mean, let's revisit two definitions mentioned earlier: selling versus branding. Selling is the process of asking a person to make a move on what you marketed to them by taking an action, such as by clicking "buy" online or by presenting cash for an in-person purchase. Selling is transactional.

Branding is what others think of you. While you may be able to influence customers' perceptions by marketing, branding comes when customers remember you for the experience of doing business with you and for the value you provide. As I wrote in my blog on Medium, "Branding is not what you say about your company, or your logo, or your tag line. Branding is really the perception your customers have about you, and the value they feel they have received from your product or service. Branding is what other people say about your business. When put in that context, it becomes important that you are clear about what you deliver and that you deliver what you say you will deliver. It is vital to have an open relationship with customers, employees, and stakeholders. It's not easy to do.

> If you're selling products, narrowing down your ideal audience is critical to making marketing decisions.

"I challenge you to think about what others say about your brand. From that, you could draw conclusions about the values, ideals, and services" your brand stands for.[1]

While marketing and selling both involve building customer relationships, they represent two different cycles. If you're selling products, narrowing down your ideal audience is critical to making marketing decisions.

During my early perfume venture, I learned that it takes a trained eye to recognize why someone is interested in your product. Is it a husband looking for a gift for his wife? Is it a woman who wants something new? Is it a daughter looking for a Mother's Day present? The sales possibilities are endless if you understand your ideal audience and how to market to them by recognizing their "why."

Knowing who you're selling to—companies or individuals—is important when identifying your seven prospective customers in the 7-7-7 Marketing process. The following table outlines typical business transactions:

B2B Business to Business	**B2C** Business to Consumer	**B2M** Business to Manufacturer
B2G Business to Government	**B2E** Business to E-Commerce	A combination of these

According to Investopedia, the "B2B e-commerce market topped $1.134 trillion—above the $954 billion it had projected for 2018 in a forecast released in 2017. That's roughly 12% of the total $9 trillion in total US B2B sales for the year." The percentage is expected to climb 17 percent by 2023.[2]

Assessing resources based on your marketing

Once you understand what type of consumer your product attracts, the next step is knowing how that affects the type and distribution of your resources. If you are a B2B, for instance, study the metrics of your ideal audience:

- **Analyze your customers' location.** Where are your customers? Are they online, right around the corner, or do they have an hour-long commute to reach you? Location-based marketing, such as direct mailers through the U.S. Post Office, can narrow this scope for you.

- **Assess delivery systems.** Do you rely on delivery or freight? Do you depend on specific vendors? How you manage this area of your business is critical. Are you agile enough to manage a supply chain disruption? Smart businesses are changing their processes to move forward. Digitization is part of building a sturdy supply chain. According to Entrepreneur.com, "As businesses adapt to the new normal, they must future-proof their supply chains by reducing complexity and uncertainties."[3] Digital tools such as data analytics, artificial intelligence, block chain, and supplier partnerships will help businesses manage supply chains, the article says.[4]

- **Consider the size of your business.** Do you have enough capacity to meet your customers' needs? Have you planned for a crisis? According to the blog post "How to apply manufacturing capacity planning in your business" by Katana, "product capacity planning ensures that you always have enough raw materials and products needed to complete an order. Raw material management is key to product capacity planning, and multi level bill of materials (BOM) are especially important if your products require a lot of product variants and subassemblies."[5]

- **Be customer-centric.** What do they want you to emphasize about your product? Do you build your marketing around your customers? Do you build your campaigns around them? Find common threads in your work with previous customers. Understanding how people worked with you in the past can help define what your future marketing should look like.

A word about automation

Many entrepreneurs are intent on automating their products or services. What our team at International Strategic Management (ISM) has discovered is that you need technologists on the team as you pursue automation. You can contract with someone to get employees up to speed on specific software. As an alternative, identify technical-leaning employees who don't mind upskilling in this area.

Either way, the person assigned to an in-house automation process can tell you what the business needs. The collaboration will be an opportunity to strengthen team relationships.

Hopefully, the same person who led the team toward automation will be there to manage the process going forward. Automation can support you scaling up in a measurable way. It also helps when you plan for automation to think about digitizing your business, from materials to content.

Don't forget your timeline

It's an excellent practice to keep a detailed record of the type of marketing you're utilizing, how much it's costing, and when and where you're marketing. Your timeline is especially important. Are you rolling out in seven days, seven weeks, or seven months, as seen in the 7-7-7 Marketing process?

What do your long- and short-term goals look like? To get started, here's a table to organize your marketing efforts:

Co. Name	Month 1	Month 2	Month 3	Month 4	Month 5	Month 6	Month 7	Notes
	Call	Drop off item	Invite to a trade show	Send an article or a blog post	Send an email	Send a Postcard	Send a letter	Change as needed
ABC								
DEF								
GHI								
JKL								
MNO								
PQR								
XYZ								

This is just one way to organize your marketing plan. Adjust the order in which you reach out based on the company's responsiveness, whether it's one individual with a primary stake in the company or a general reply from an administrative assistant or office manager.

You can customize this table as needed for your company. If you're working with small businesses, it may be beneficial to tailor your marketing to each business so they feel they're valued. It all depends on your vision.

If you're struggling to conceptualize a plan like this, at ISM we've seen a great many individuals initially tell us this does not work for them. After a few conversations, however, they realize that it's all for them, actually! So, don't struggle and stop. We offer several customized resources and plans that many have used to take their businesses to the next level.

A FINJAN MOMENT 

Preparation is everything. Have you prepared your business for a crisis so that you can continue serving customers?

ACTION

Write descriptions of your products. Are they customer-centric?

"Learning to ask the right questions can drive and create opportunities. I've discovered, working with entrepreneurs and leaders, that questions which seem simple — or even sound dumb — can actually be intriguing and cause you to think deeper." — Faris Alami on "How Questions Drive Opportunities"

CHAPTER 8
PROVIDING SERVICES

Perhaps you're feeling intimidated by the thought of finding seven people willing to accept your service. I get it. Reaching out to strangers can be difficult, even with the strong possibility that one day they will become customers or even friends. Again, let's review the basics. Don't doubt that you can *provide* a service. However, strenuously question *why* people would want your service, *who* you will serve, and *how* you will serve them.

The next step would be to create a profile of your ideal audience. For example, if you are a carpet-cleaning company, list homeowners in specific zip codes, medical office leasing agents, and apartment complexes. Consider your services carefully here. Services any entrepreneur offers are provided within a social, cultural, educational, and economic context. How well you understand your ideal audience plays a role in the return on your investment. In other words, does your ideal audience want what you're selling?

Does your ideal audience want what you're selling?

Redefine your ideal audience

It may seem smarter to go wide and reach as many people as possible, but wider can become a scattershot effort if your target is imprecise. It's simply not true that *everyone* you see is a prospect. As an entrepreneur, define a specific customer type you'll pursue to ensure they buy from you because they benefit the most from your product or service.

Narrow down your ideal audience: they are the group you can serve. You know this ideal audience needs what you provide, and you may have determined that by studying geographic locations or demographics, for example. However, if a few customers come to your door who don't fit your specifications for an ideal customer, that's a blessing. Celebrate when they come into the fold but understand they're not the typical audience you plan to serve.

Let's illustrate that idea further with another example. You remodel homes. Have you overlooked other people or businesses that might require your service? What's the customer profile of those who have used your service in the past? Do you have a specialty as a remodeler? Maybe you can trick out a master bathroom like no one else. Is your expertise in luxury baths or efficient and safe master bathrooms for seniors? Will you focus on reaching residents in homes with a certain square footage in specific zip codes? Will you target houses of a certain age and construction type? Do you get where I'm going with all these questions? If you do, your next step is to think of seven ways to *interact* with the people in those categories.

As an example, here are a few ideas for the remodeling business. As the business owner, you could enroll in a mailer service such as Val-Pac or Using Every Door Direct Mail from USPS in which you can:

- Offer a DIY article in exchange for their email address
- Offer birthday discounts!
- Invite them to an exhibit you have at a trade show
- Connect with other services or business owners to create a referral program

- Post how-to videos and give special offers to subscribers to your channel
- Display your work on Instagram and link to seasonal offers
- Attend home events and trade shows
- Become an expert source for realtors

Create a time frame

Will you complete this outreach in seven days, seven weeks, or seven months? Define your short- and long-term outreach goals. This should be a logical step because when you plan your business, you must set short- and long-term goals. It may be helpful to review Chapter Three, where I discuss creating ways to reach customers over time.

If you're struggling to formulate this on your own, we would be honored to assign one of our professionals to work alongside you to support you and help create your business plan. We have programs that can walk you through the process, or we can implement a plan for you. There are also plenty of targeted advertising programs online.

Here's an example of a table you could use to organize your marketing strategies:

Zip Code	Week 1	Week 2	Week 3	Week 4	Week 5	Week 6	Week 7	Notes
	Mailer	Postcard	Flier	Invite to home trade show	Mail a DYI article	Different postcard	Door -to- door activity	Change as needed
12345								
12346								
12347								
12349								
12349								

This type of organization and marketing plan can be applied to many different types of businesses and services. If you find it difficult to think of seven different types of target audiences, I recommend “zooming out” on the prospects.

Let’s go back to the carpet-cleaning business example. In this case, there are many ways to break down your ideal audience. Start by thinking of types of businesses to reach in your marketing:

- Professional offices
- Geographical areas (zip codes, as noted above)
- Medical offices
- Schools/day care centers
- Neighborhoods/HOAs

If you’re still struggling to understand how to apply these steps to your business as a service provider, don’t hesitate to reach out to my firm, International Strategic Management (ISM), to receive individualized attention for your business. My team offers plenty of resources to gain momentum in marketing your services.

A FINJAN MOMENT 

Good questions offer a bumper crop of new insights. Sometimes, questions we receive from those not in our industry can provide even more powerful information.

ACTION

Study the services you offer. Plot your customer's journey like a mini-movie. What do you see in the customer's journey? What can be tweaked to heighten customer satisfaction?

“The more specific you are about your customer, the bigger your market becomes.” — Faris Alami on “The 6 domains of the Entrepreneurship Ecosystem: Part Two — Markets”

CHAPTER 9
MARKET SEGMENTATION

Knowing the segments in which your customers fall is the first step in creating appropriate marketing strategies for each of them. One of our older International Strategic Management (ISM) posts captures the idea of segmentation quite well:

"The adage, 'Don't put all your eggs in one basket' applies to almost every aspect of our lives and businesses and is especially true in the marketing arena. Segmenting your markets—breaking typical customers down into several precise demographic groups—is a great way to spread your marketing dollars (your 'eggs') across groups of people with different needs in a very focused, precise manner."[1]

Segmenting your markets—breaking typical customers down into several demographic groups—is a great way to spread your marketing dollars (your "eggs") across groups of people with different needs in a very focused, precise manner.

Categorizing customers into marketing segments boosts business; it doesn't diminish it. Segmentation creates ways to address the needs of specific customers, thus leading to more satisfied customers. For example, let's say you own a bike shop. One customer fancies touring bikes, another favors folding bikes, another adores mountain bikes, and another can't get through a weekend without their BMX bike. Do you market to them in the same way? Yes and no. In the general sense, they're all bikers. But each biker has different preferences when it comes to the riding experience. Questions about speed and accessories will differ. Your job is to know what each customer group needs and tell that story in your marketing.

Some entrepreneurs may pursue a one-size-fits-all marketing approach, and you can pursue that if you choose;

however, I recommend studying your customers and learning how they use your product. Their preferences will give you insights into how to reach them specifically and more effectively.

Here are four ways to think of market segmentation in this chart from that blog post.[2]

Geographic: region, by city, by zip code, by neighborhood	Demographic: age, gender, occupation, etc.	Psychographic: lifestyle, values, interests, beliefs	Behavioral: Product use or benefits, brand loyalty

The four segments can be broken down even further:

Gender	Age	Lifestyle	Disposable income	Community interests[3]

Again, use market segmentation to be specific when wooing your customers. Lots of gems can be discovered in this space. As I wrote in the blog post "Market Segments," "The broader you are, the fewer customers will be interested in you. The more focused you are, the more customers will be interested in you. In other words: When you are for *everyone*, no one comes; when you are for *someone*, everyone comes."[4]

A FINJAN MOMENT 

Think about how you can break down your market into segments so that you can dig deeper into each one and create marketing materials that support your segment.

ACTION

What do you offer customers that no one else can?

"You must always be thinking about how to improve your results." — Faris Alami on "Analyze Your Results"

CHAPTER 10
SALES NUMBERS

Sales numbers.

You may cringe at the words, but running a business means numbers connect with everything you do or aspire to achieve. It doesn't matter whether you keep the books, your bookkeeper, CPA, or favorite uncle do: sales numbers reveal the story of your business.

They unveil what's happening in the background or foreground because sales numbers are the eyes and ears of your enterprise.

Because my 7-7-7 Marketing requires a full understanding of your business and its impact on your customers, keeping track of sales numbers is critical. Documenting sales numbers clarifies your marketing efforts and enables you to respond to critical business shifts like the following:

- More employee hours are required before you reach sales targets

- There are not enough weekly customer purchases to make a profit after expenses

- The monthly email newsletter converts more customers than the expensive highway billboard

- You're producing too many cupcakes every day; they're spoiling because you only promote your sandwiches

- Your oil lube appointments increase when you promote them with a $5 Starbucks card

- Customers prefer your freshly made pasta with basil, not the boxed, no-name brand you thought would cut costs

- You resist it, but you need to hire another employee because customers are complaining about long lines and your pharmacy team is racking up outrageous overtime every week

- One guest appearance you made on a podcast about clothing led to more visits to your website and converted more sales than a traditional ad did in a month

- Customer service calls have jumped ten percent for two years straight because of bugs in your mobile app

An in-depth financial understanding of your business means understanding the cost of goods or services sold, the profit margin, and much more. For example, when you compare current sales against those in a previous month, or a previous year, you spot changes in your business performance. Each detail becomes a key indicator as you learn what's profitable, what customers crave, and what they ignore. All of it matters.

Sales numbers guide you in stocking your shelves, organizing a conference more expertly, pursuing specific customers, adjusting marketing campaigns, choosing different media platforms to sell your products or services, and upskilling your sales team.

Forced to change

Let's go back to my business career again. Remember my perfume business? I worked all day—from 8:00 a.m. to 10:00 p.m.—without a single sale to show for it. Eventually, I had to acknowledge that while I worked with all my might, I failed because my efforts weren't the sales efforts that yielded results. Worst of all, it took me years to learn the right way to achieve robust sales.

As I have said repeatedly in person and in my blog posts, I learned that I needed to speak with about ten people before selling once.[1] I changed my approach, increased my interactions with customers, and my sales numbers grew. Transactions rose from nothing to multiple transactions daily—and upward to fifty transactions. And when I went into retail, my sales efforts reached thousands of transactions every day. Being forced to change how I interacted with customers transformed my business. When I learned to increase my interactions with people, I stopped being disappointed when customers dismissed my products. I realized that I just hadn't met the right customer yet.

> When I learned to increase my interaction with people, I stopped being disappointed when customers dismissed my products. I realized I hadn't met the right customer yet.

Let me add a footnote here. If a customer shows a sustained disinterest in your offer, don't persuade them. Don't be that salesperson. A wiser move is to answer questions politely, thank the person for their time, and move on to the next person who may be excited about your product or service because it fulfills their needs. In the eyes of your ideal customer, when you two connect, it's *the* interaction they've been waiting for!

Sales tracking tools

Find a viable method of tracking your sales numbers. If you're still growing, you can use that old but faithful tool, Excel. You can also try Google Sheets. There are also many other CRM tools you can choose from, such as:

- Zoho
- Salesforce
- HubSpot

A final thought. You can use these tools to check conversion rates, which can reveal a great deal about your sales process and marketing efforts. Be willing to learn where your money really comes from, whether you're charging enough, and how you typically generate customer prospects. The horizon where sales goals line up and wait remains very blurry until you put in the appropriate sales efforts, reach the ideal customer, and track sales numbers—the compass that steers you toward your business goals.

A FINJAN MOMENT 

Spending too much time trying to educate a customer about the benefits of a product or service can waste precious sales energy. Stay on the lookout for those who need what you offer.

ACTION

Do you track your sales activities? What have been the results?

"One of the things we've learned by watching entrepreneurs and leaders around the globe is that while they love to compete with others, most of the time, they are competing with themselves." — *Faris Alami on "Compete with Yourself"*

CHAPTER 11
IMPLEMENTING YOUR MARKETING PLAN

While the 7-7-7 Marketing process I've discussed in this book supplements what you're doing in your business, it's an invaluable addition. I encourage you to keep doing what you're doing—putting in the time to improve your products and services, learning more about entrepreneurship and seeking mentors—as you implement 7-7-7 Marketing into your business every day.

Remember, 7-7-7 Marketing focuses on building relationships with your customers rather than just closing a sale. Aiming for sales alone is a transactional mindset and brings short-term value to your business. While sales lead to more money for your business, a relationship mindset will secure the future of your business and solidify the long-term stability of your client base. Relationships keep people coming back for more of what you offer.

Executing your strategy

After you finish the initial setup and map out your marketing plan, start executing your strategy. This process should not take more than a few hours a week, if you allocate, say, one hour per week to it.

When I first implemented this process, I set aside time early in the morning, when the office was quiet. I asked myself the hard questions. Where could I improve? Was I on track with my goals? What had become familiar but unprofitable? That time of solitude was always fruitful for me.

Don't be afraid to adjust as needed

Change is real. Trends emerge, businesses move, and customer expectations evolve. When this happens, customize the seven ways you contact a customer. Markets may change, but imagination runs free within the parameters of 7-7-7 Marketing. Use change to refine the ways you reach your target audience. If something isn't working for one business, try something new!

Be there

One of the most powerful ways to stay relevant in the business world is to make sure your contacts know you're available. Consistent marketing, whether direct or indirect, keeps your products and services visible. Offer an email newsletter with relevant content, announce special offers on social media, and participate in events where you serve the community. Be present for your customers, serve them authentically, and they'll remember you when they're ready to buy.

Your digital footprint

Entrepreneurs must have a digital footprint. This relates to what I discussed earlier about being available. Hang your shingle to show you're open for business on the internet by displaying a basic online presence:

- A professional company email address
- A website or landing page
- A social media presence
- Follow up with potential customers online with content

This doesn't have to be complex. These steps can be part of a smaller task list you can tackle based on your company's priorities. For example, an email address with your name and company name adds legitimacy, as does a mailing address. (Of course, relationships overcome all of this, but it helps you to set up your digital presence.) Add multiple email addresses as needed when you a buy a domain name.

Change is real. Trends emerge, businesses move, and customer expectations evolve.

Websites can be extensive or merely one-pagers with a description of your services and contact information. In due course, you can add more services and products. You can also redirect your domain name to your Facebook business page.

Choose what social presence works for you but don't be afraid to experiment. Find out what makes you comfortable. How often do you want to interact on your selected platform? Have a strategy for how often you will post. This will help your business carry a weightier and consistent presence on social media.

Lastly, create an email newsletter, online course, or an online group to engage customers and promote your business. These steps can be carried out over time to ensure a major impact at a low cost.

Marketing metrics

Once you gather details about your ideal customer and the sales cycle process, you can create a marketing dashboard. It doesn't have to be elaborate. You can record data in an Excel worksheet. You will gain a deeper understanding of your business and can include metrics like these:

- How many people do you need to talk to before they walk into the store? This includes questions such as: how many fliers do you need to pass out? How many ads? And how many trade shows must you attend?

- How many potential customers from the trade show qualify for follow-up?

- How often should you follow up with them?

- If you run a text message marketing campaign, how many times do you have to touch them before they buy online or walk in your store? How many days, weeks, or months does it take?

- How many customers are needed to support one of your salespeople?

Once you get accustomed to collecting data about your business, you can use Microsoft Power BI or a visualization tool like Tableau to query and analyze information quickly. Some best practices for choosing a solid tool include the following considerations:

- Determine who will manage or use the marketing dashboard

- Research vendors to determine which company fits your business needs and budget

- Study vendors' privacy policies to ensure your data isn't compromised

- Get a real-time view of the data or reports you require

It may be time-consuming to capture data, but you gain a measurable idea of how your business performs. Metrics can be retrieved from any part of your business. They help you uncover inefficiencies in your operations, customer preferences, customer service, resource gaps, spending, and much more.

When you know how your business runs, and when it's running at optimum performance, you're able to mitigate issues much sooner. You're also better prepared for occasions when you're required to discuss your business in detail, such as when you're raising capital for expansion. Each detail you gather will count.

Competition

The marketplace tends to create an us-versus-them environment. Sometimes you're forced to compete—and that's okay. However, I choose to cooperate whenever possible. Being willing to cooperate doesn't translate to thinking small. It's actually thinking big! Let me go one step further with this idea of cooperation. I encourage you to collaborate with your competition. Wild, right? But hear me out. I'm asking you to search for a competitor and to support them. Incredibly, a customer base can grow in that type of cross-pollinated environment among competitors with complementary businesses.

When you support competitors, many things can happen. Your market share can grow. A competitor may buy you out at an irresistible price. And here's a thrilling idea: one day *you* may buy them out! Many entrepreneurs have taken this leap and employed this strategy with success. Could you be next?

A FINJAN MOMENT 

Race against yourself for the best sales numbers. See yourself as the competition. In time, don't be surprised by this silver lining: you find your business in a wider field of play with larger companies.

ACTION

Summarize your thoughts about what you learned. What goals do you want to pursue?

"Don't let others mislead you about what success is in your life or business. Success is not having a car. It is not taking a vacation. It is not having a million dollars in the bank.

Actually, it may be all of those things to some people. Success for one person might be having a one-bedroom apartment, while to others, a 1,000 square foot house is the measure. Each of us should be able to define success in our own way." — Faris Alami on "The Challenge of Defining Success"

CHAPTER 12
NOW, IT'S YOUR TURN

Congratulations! By going through this book and thinking about the 7-7-7 Marketing strategy, you're ready to assess what you've learned. Getting educated about marketing and other aspects of business won't matter if you don't allow the ideas to settle in.

Reflection is extremely useful for entrepreneurs. When you set aside time to put a mirror up to your work, to your ideas—and any other area of life, for that matter—you gain perspective about your challenges and find new ways to manage a business project.

As stated in the International Strategic Management (ISM) blog post "Leadership: Self-Governance & Reflection," taking time to slow down and assess can provide you with a fresh crop of ideas about your business:[1]

"The skill set of self-governance sparks many of the innovations and results that we see today. As you govern your body, your tasks, and vision or mission, as you control what you do every day, it becomes clear why you should be motivated every morning."[2]

This chapter is an opportunity to practice self-governance, to wrangle ideas about your business, to assess what works and what doesn't. In that process, you may discover deeper truths about your life that can benefit you personally and speed up your success as an entrepreneur.

This chapter is an opportunity to practice self-governance, to wrangle ideas about your business, to assess what works and what doesn't.

Using brainstorming prompts

It can be helpful to create a distraction-free zone where you allow yourself to think about a range of business possibilities. I invite you to regularly use brainstorming as a tool to resolve a resource problem or examine a difficult challenge differently. If you brainstorm with your team, you expand the chance of problem solving exponentially because you gain the opportunity to hear ideas from everyone.

Asking whether you have everything you need and whether there are any other approaches you can take is an invaluable session for you. Questions can be business-related or personal. Take as much time as you need, or plan for multiple sessions where you can brainstorm. I encourage you to use an array of available brainstorming tools, including but not limited to MindMeister, Coggle, LucidChart, and Bit.ai. Of course, there's always room for whiteboards and sticky notes!

The more time you spend building the foundations of your business, the better prepared you will be to serve customers, calculate and forecast sales, and track the soundness of your enterprise.

Business planning

We discussed business planning in Chapter Four. In this step, I'll pose another list of questions. You must choose whether you wish to read the questions and take notes, but I encourage you to do so: writing your answers may trigger other ideas. Set aside sufficient time to do so, whether alone or with your team.

Before you begin, I suggest looking at a few facts about the costs of starting a business. The Small Business Administration's Office of Advocacy Small Business Finance FAQ provides numerous insights you can consider when brainstorming about your business.[3] Here are a few to consider:

- "The financing needs of small businesses vary greatly by employer and non-employer firms and by age and industry. According to the Federal Reserve Banks, in 2020, the share of employer firms seeking financing was 37%. 24% of nonemployer firms sought financing. Only 37% of employer firms received the full amount sought in 2020. 29% of larger nonemployer firms received full funding, compared to only 17% of smaller nonemployer firms in 2020.[4]

- "Business financing comes from numerous sources categorized either as internal (family and friends/personal savings) or external (bank loans). Existing businesses often use retained business earnings. 77% of businesses used business earnings as their primary source of funding in 2019, compared with 64% in 2016.[5]

- "New business financing options typically fall into two categories: debt and equity. New business owners often depend on their own resources for start-up capital. 75% of new businesses use personal savings while 19% report using a bank loan for startup capital. Unconventional sources can also play a critical role in meeting a firm's financial needs. 17% of new employer businesses report using credit cards.[6]

- "Like other businesses, women-owned employer firms use a wide range of capital to start. 41% of women business owners tend to start with capital amounts [of] less than $10,000. Women are less likely to use bank loans compared to their male counterparts. This may put women-owned firms at a disadvantage since an early relationship with a bank may be critical for future business financing. About 13.1% of women-owned ventures did not use any funding compared to 11.5% of male-owned ventures."[7]

The facts are sobering. Knowing how things stand in business can reveal how much help you need to get started. At ISM, we're always willing to help entrepreneurs fully grasp the financial picture of their businesses. Because we gained so much information from working with amazing entrepreneurs and leaders, it's helped us support even more entrepreneurs.

Here are more questions for your written business plan that I encourage you to consider. Again, the more precise you are in your planning, the better prepared you are:

General information: Have you developed a detailed plan that provides information, such as a company description, your market, the marketing and sales plan, your management team, a financial summary, and an investor summary?

Marketing plan: How much depth do you give to your marketing plan? Do you define an industry profile for the reader that includes trends as well as your growth potential? Do you discuss direct, indirect, and future competition? Do you take extensive time to develop a customer profile?

Products and services: When you define your product or service, how specific are you? Do you have a proof of concept? Can you indicate its stage of development? Are copyrights needed for intellectual property? What about government approvals? Are there any liabilities or limitations that should be mentioned? Is the product or service ready or still in production? Who are your suppliers and how reliable are they?

Pricing: Do you address your pricing strategy comprehensively? Do you have a solid price list? Are there written policies attached? Have you analyzed what breaking even looks like for your business?

Business sales and performance

In Chapter Five we discussed the life cycle of a business and in Chapter Six the sales cycle. I often highlight with entrepreneurs that they should manage their numbers daily. I'm not talking about tax-time management when you rush to gather financial documentation for your CPA and the IRS. I'm talking about gaining a core understanding of what it costs for you to make your product or provide your service.

Take a moment to calculate *the true cost* of your business. Poor estimates and false assumptions about what it may take to make a sale can be devastating to a business. When we don't have a handle on our numbers, we could be paying others to do business with us!

I suggest you know the numbers for these four categories: a) sales and marketing; b) operations; c) financial forms; and d) forecasts and potential funding. While you have an accountant and other financial professionals to assist you, knowing the financial state of your business carries many benefits and can open unexpected doors.

You can plot your success more accurately when knowing what it costs to go from wooing clients to getting them to buy. Who knows? Possessing a working knowledge of what it costs to operate your business from staffing to production costs may get you noticed by an angel investor if you can explain what your reasonable forecasts are. (Of course, this also means you can correctly interpret and discuss the financial documents from your CPA!)

No one should know your business better than you. Become skilled in how to track your numbers. Run numbers daily, weekly, and monthly for the four categories I mentioned so that you can truly be at the helm of your business. Finance, funding, projections, and many more topics are involved here. I hope this gets you thinking about the financial aspects of your business planning.

Technology

SEO (Search Engine Optimization), VPNs (Virtual Private Networks), APIs (Application Programming Interfaces) may be unfamiliar terms, but you need to have a basic grasp of them and of many others. As Neil Cumin writes in his short but informative post in Business News Daily, "Technology Terms Every Entrepreneur Should Know,"

"There are certain technology terms every entrepreneur should know that will help them understand the evolving tech sector and its role in their business."[8]

Emerging technologies assist entrepreneurs in tremendous ways. However, despite the productivity and efficiency these technologies provide, there are risks as well as mandatory compliance standards required for businesses handling customer data. Get up to speed on what you need to do so that you can protect your business and the customer data you may collect and manage.

This space is constantly changing, and it's the environment where you must conduct business, whether you own a mid-town cookie shop or operate a pottery store on Shopify. You'll need to protect customer data and your own. You'll need to strive for a frictionless experience for your customers when they navigate your website and mobile apps. So, if you need it, seek help from professionals with expertise in cybersecurity, software engineering, data science, the user experience, and related fields to make brainstorming in this area meaningful for you.

If you're a young entrepreneur, you can join us in the nonprofit Connecting the Dots Globally program, where our activities include working with high school and college students to become STEMpreneurs in the areas of science, technology, engineering, and math.[9] To date, we've worked with over 5,000 young people worldwide. The goal is to help them learn how to launch global technology companies. I also invite you to join us if you are an entrepreneur or organization that wants to support young STEMpreneurs. Your insights and wisdom will be invaluable!

A FINJAN MOMENT

My mom always said, "patience is beautiful." It's so true! As you consider your future steps as an entrepreneur, never forget patience. Remembering this simple statement will come in handy when you feel pressed to seek unreasonable goals from those around you.

ACTION

What are your goals for the short or long term? What's the realistic and patience-filled timetable you can create from what you've learned?

"What has come clear to me over my years of supporting organizations and entrepreneurs is that entrepreneurship is a mindset. It's not about putting payroll on a credit card, or taking risks, although sometimes those things are a part of it. The main thing about the mindset is how you look for a problem, provide a solution, or look for an opportunity to provide some value." — Faris Alami, "What is an Entrepreneur?"

CHAPTER 13
MOVE WITH CONFIDENCE

This is it. You've reached the end of this book. I hope you have assessed your marketing strategy and integrated the approaches offered in 7-7-7 Marketing. My deepest hope is that this book pivots you from running an ordinary business to managing an extraordinary enterprise that empowers your team and serves your customers and community.

The triumphs and pitfalls of building a business are legendary. Who hasn't heard of entrepreneurs creating multi-billion-dollar enterprises with bold ideas but little money? And, of course, who hasn't heard of large businesses that were stock market darlings that tumbled hard—for all to see?

What I've discovered as an entrepreneur—and after working with entrepreneurs and the organizations that support them—is that building a business is a testing ground. In no time at all, an array of circumstances can try entrepreneurs by fire. The pressure to give up will be great. Refuse to allow hard times to immobilize you. Use those hard times to ask questions, to probe for solutions.

Unfortunately, for some entrepreneurs, the recurring temptation is to quit because they don't have enough experience. At some point in their life, someone told them that they lacked what it takes to be entrepreneurs. Carrying that mindset becomes a breeding ground of doubt and frustration. Experience has advantages and it does open doors, but experience isn't the only road to business success and should never be viewed as a showstopper. Believe me, if you pull up in the parking lot with your food truck during lunch hour at a busy office building, the game is still on.

Experience has advantages, and it does open doors, but experience isn't the only road to business success and should never be viewed as a showstopper.

Over the years I've worked with under-served, under-represented, and under-resourced communities, and I've seen how they've pushed ahead to grow a business without what an educational institution or an industry would describe as genuine experience. What these entrepreneurs had going for them was the strong desire to solve a problem in their community or to fulfill a need. Had they heeded the naysayers instead of following their personal vision and relying on their strength, the lack of a lengthy resume would have stifled the gifts they eventually brought their communities.

At every stage of the entrepreneurial game, you will have the chance to transform problems into opportunity, leverage resources to move forward, and push to be thoughtful, compassionate, and visionary. Get ready!

Prepare, prepare, prepare

With preparation, the road to entrepreneurship becomes easy to navigate. Whether you envision a small, bustling, and profitable coffee shop or a multi-billion-dollar global enterprise employing thousands, preparation is fundamental. Preparation expects roadblocks, shores up for mishaps, and positions you to learn more.

Preparation is like plot points in a story. What story does your business tell? What are the dramatic reveals? Whether you run a startup or a legacy business organization, there should be a narrative, one that you create every day you sell your product or service.

"But Faris," you may ask, "what does storytelling have to do with my business? I own a dry-cleaning business. Not a Starbucks."

I understand your perspective. I really do. Storytelling has everything to do with it, though. How you perceive your business and demonstrate what you perceive tells a story to every customer, vendor, and competitor. You care just because you do! *This is your story.* However, if you think you merely operate a dry-cleaning business, you're right. That's all you have. There's no distinction, no pride of ownership that you care for people's clothes like they're your own, that you take the time to get to know your customers even when they don't have a garment to dry clean. I encourage you to aim high. Plot your business story and tell it well.

Unexpected benefits of storytelling

Storytelling may also take you into conversations you never expected. Our research at International Strategic Management (ISM) shows that a compelling narrative about why you're in business influences potential investors. Entrepreneurs with a story about why they need funding and who can cite for how long and how they plan to allocate the funds, are most often successful in gaining nontraditional funding. Ignite the storyteller within you. It matters!

A trouble-free business isn't guaranteed

I can't promise you your business won't go through rough periods. Some troubles might begin immediately and may last for weeks and months, possibly longer. Droughts in foot traffic because of delays on a street construction project may cool sales for months at your clothing boutique in that up-and-coming neighborhood. Inflation may make customers reluctant to buy your products in an uncertain market. A new competitor may come to your block with little interest in collaborating and the obvious intent of putting you out of business.

Such occurrences aren't unusual for entrepreneurs to endure and overcome. I've encountered them in my own business career. Instead of my entrepreneurial journey beginning in a college business class or at the family shoe store in a sleepy downtown, remember my story. My first business lessons emerged from life-and-death struggles in a war zone. Looking back, each step forward required resilience, relentless observation, and relating to people's needs.

Over the past thirty years, I've learned from my experiences and gleaned insights from the wonderful entrepreneurs and leaders I either supported or worked with. I learned from school and a variety of settings and scenarios in over one hundred countries and in more than eighty industries. I've been blessed to travel over 1.2 million miles to places I never would have imagined visiting earlier in my life. I studied business practices during formal meetings at a tech firm—and every time my mechanic gave my car an oil change.

Business success is a process

But like you, even as my business matured, I faced highs and the lows; there were seasons when I was flooded with the word "yes" and others when I heard "no" after "no" after "no." Through it all, what have I learned? I've learned that business is a process. Planning who you will contact and how you will do so demands work. Beefing up your networking skills, mastering the life cycle of a business, studying your sales cycle, implementing a strong business plan, and understanding customer segmentation: all of these take effort.

That's the nature of entrepreneurship. You're always learning something new. You're always growing.

Be confident in your ability to reach people with your goods and services. Believe that your ideal customer needs what you produce. In gratitude serve others as customers, friends, and community. I promise you this: benefits will come from this approach in ways you never expected. For decades, many people have asked me to speak on the topics I share in this book. While in the past I would never have thought of myself as an entrepreneur or leader, it has become my responsibility to own what I am. You see, owning my gifts and expressing them with humility and confidence has been a journey for me as well.

Marketing is personal

Shoddy, random marketing efforts usually fail and damage your customer relationships. Low energy and unprofessional efforts in marketing will affect your branding, advertising, and distribution efforts—so it's important to get it right.

When I reflect on my career as an entrepreneur, and having supported other businesses and entrepreneurs through ISM, I'm grateful to have developed a marketing approach people can apply to an array of companies and industries. I think it works because marketing is personal. Marketing will reveal your attitude toward people. You treat people based on the mindset and heart attitude you carry. I encourage you to carry a positive vibe!

As I often share with entrepreneurs, it's not what happens to you that matters: it's your reaction to those circumstances. I've seen this played out in war zones and difficult regions where my team has worked. Attitude determines results. Attitude fuels your ascent from the bottom to the top. Keep your attitude positive and make it a habit of remaining uplifted and teachable: the best days of your entrepreneurial journey are yet to come.

A FINJAN MOMENT

When your business grows, keep asking yourself questions. Allow yourself to be uncomfortable. Stretch yourself!

ACTION

Entrepreneurs have told us that having an advisory board or mentor increased their business revenue. Name those who can walk alongside you.

RESOURCES

By reading this book, you've started your 7-7-7 Marketing journey. I wish you much success! When you're ready for further training, please visit International Strategic Management (ISM) online to get professional assistance. Here's a snapshot curated from our site for a few of our most popular workshops and programs.[1]

ISM Signature Workshops include the following:

The Power of Marketing introduces a proven and successful marketing tool, called Marketing, as you design your marketing strategy. Participants learn the importance of contact and the three main steps to establish contact with customers: 1) create your customer list, 2) schedule your contact dates, and 3) choose your contact method.

The Art of Effective Networking introduces five key skills that make connecting simple and natural: Planning, Active Listening, Asking Strategic Questions, Focusing on the Other Person, and Adding Value. This immersive session emphasizes learning-by-doing. Participants will leave with the tools, plans, activities, and work-products they can immediately use at home or in the workplace.

From Start-up to Scale-up introduces proven tools for approaching problems and opportunities, and how to leverage the resources you have rather than those you need. This immersive workshop emphasizes learning-by-doing. Participants learn the following: when a start-up becomes a scale-up, the scale-up viability of the business, scaling efforts in sync with the rest of the operation, the strength of your core product/service, which marketing channels give you the highest ROI, the execution team, and accessing the cash to scale up.

How to Ask for Money introduces the skills you need to learn to ask someone to fund your business: clarity about your current status, communication, information sharing, and honesty. Participants learn about the various types of investors, what to ask, and how to explain your business model, including what you've accomplished, what needs to happen next, and the total amount of money to ask for depending on the time frame of operations and how long this fund will sustain your business.

ISM Signature Programs include the following:

Entrepreneurial Ecosystem Development © is a 12-month program in which participants come to understand the components of the ecosystem, showcase with other ecosystem players, and launch a few programs that ignite the entrepreneurship culture.

Global Entrepreneurship and Leadership Accelerator Program © is a three-month cohort-style entrepreneurship program targeting startups already engaged in the entrepreneurial ecosystem in their home country, such as being part of incubation or acceleration programs.

Resilient Entrepreneur © This high-impact five-week program is offered in two formats: A self-education course (beginner, professional, and elite) and a virtual in-person course.

Chart your course

The charts below can help you navigate this method and provide a foundation for the beginning of your 7-7-7 Marketing journey. Customize them. Make them work for you as you strategize to reach your ideal customer.

A. YOUR "DREAM" CLIENT AND CUSTOMER CHART

Potential Customer	Touch 1	Touch 2	Touch 3	Touch 4	Touch 5	Touch 6	Touch 7

B. YOUR "COULD BE" CLIENT AND CUSTOMER CHART

Potential Customer	Touch 1	Touch 2	Touch 3	Touch 4	Touch 5	Touch 6	Touch 7

C. YOUR "SHOULD BE" CLIENT AND CUSTOMER CHART

Potential Customer	Touch 1	Touch 2	Touch 3	Touch 4	Touch 5	Touch 6	Touch 7

Helpful links

myisminc.com

farisalami.com

https://www.marketingbrew.com/

https://www.bls.gov/

https://www.census.gov/

https://www.economist.com/

https://www.entrepreneur.com/

https://hbr.org/

https://www.fastcompany.com/

https://www.forbes.com/?sh=7e1715772254

https://www.wired.com/

https://www.bloomberg.com/businessweek

GLOSSARY

They say knowledge is power—so understanding business terms will play to your advantage. I hope the terms defined below will help you and also encourage you to learn more terms.

Accessibility Standards: The Americans with Disabilities Act (ADA) and the Architectural Barriers Act (ABA) issue standards that ensure buildings and facilities are accessible to those with disabilities. Learn more at https://www.access-board.gov/buildings.html

Agile: You'll hear this word often used to describe whether a business is nimble for change. You'll also hear it used as an approach for company teamwork. While an agile framework often applies to software development, many corporations incorporate Agile principles in their enterprises. For more information, go to https://www.scrum.org/

Accounts Payable: This is what you owe your creditors.

Accounts Receivable: This refers to what people owe you.

CCPA: The acronym for the California Consumer Privacy Act, enacted in 2018. This law protects how personal customer information such as browsing history, geolocation data, credit card information, and email addresses are used by for-profit businesses that conduct business in California. To learn more, visit https://oag.ca.gov/privacy/ccpa

Capital: This term has an array of meanings. One of them refers to financial assets that a business needs for liquidity to execute a business goal. When handled correctly, the more successful a company has a chance to become. For a fuller definition, go to https://www.investopedia.com/terms/c/capital.asp

CRM: Customer Relationship Management. Use this term to track technology engagement with customers and potential customers.

Entrepreneur: There is no right or wrong way to define entrepreneurship. I've flown a million miles and heard a million definitions! I want to challenge all these ideas and take us to the very crux of entrepreneurship: the *mindset* of the individual looking for an opportunity to create something or looking to solve an existing problem.

Fixed Costs: Think of business costs, such as equipment or the office space you lease.

Friction, Frictionless: Think of a mobile app. Is it too much trouble for a customer to use? Is the checkout process too long or confusing? That's *friction*. If it's easy to navigate, that's *frictionless.*

GDPR: Like the CCPA, the General Data Protection Regulation governs compliance regarding a customer's personal data online. However, the GDPR is required for organizations that do business with residents of the European Union. Organizations are required to alert users about what data is collected and how it's being used. Under the GDPR, customers have more control over how their personal data is use. For more information, visit https://gdpr-info.eu/

Gross: Your business has a total gross income of $50,000 in its first year before deductions. See **Net**.

Incentivize: You give your customers incentives to come to your store on Sunday afternoons by offering 10 percent discounts. This is *incentivizing.*

Marketing: You understand this one. You market or promote your products and services. You research your market and ideal customer. For the formal definition by the American Marketing Association, go to https://www.ama.org/the-definition-of-marketing-what-is-marketing/

Margin (accounting): According to Investopedia, this is "the difference between revenue and expenses where businesses typically track their gross profit margins, operating margins, and net profit margins." [1,2]

Metrics: These are "measures of quantitative assessment commonly used for assessing, comparing, and tracking performance or production," according to Investopedia. "Metrics have been used in accounting, operations, and performance analysis throughout history."[3]

Most Viable Product: "Minimum Viable Product." This term defines the most basic version of a product that you can launch to market.

Net: Your business has a net income of $30,000 after deducting taxes and other expenses. See **Gross**.

Niche Market: Your specialty area to serve your target audience. You meet their unique needs in this market.

Responsive Web Design: Users should be able to view your website easily and clearly on all screens and devices. Learn more about responsive design, along with free tools to test your site, at https://www.webfx.com/blog/web-design/what-is-responsive-web-design/

ROI: Return on Investment: In other words, the metric that allows you to assess what you get back when you invest time, money, and resources.

Sales Funnel: TechTarget describes a sales funnel (also purchase funnel) as "the visual representation of the customer journey, depicting the sales process from awareness to action."[4]

Scalable, Scalability: Investopedia states that "Scalability, whether it be in a financial context or within a context of business strategy, describes a company's ability to grow without being hampered by its structure or available resources when faced with increased production."[5]

SEO: Search Engine Optimization. Use key words and terms, and specific content to improve your site's visibility with search engines—a critical marketing tactic to reach customers on the web.

SWOT Analysis: Use this technique to review your company's strengths, weaknesses, opportunities, and threats.

Usability: When people come to your site, do they love it for its ease of use? If so, you have designed the website so that it has a high level of *usability*.

User experience, UX: This is the all-round experience your customers have with every facet of your company, including marketing. Learn more at https://www.nngroup.com/articles/definition-user-experience/

END NOTES

INTRODUCTION

1. https://www.history.com/this-day-in-history/iraq-invades-kuwait#:~:text=On%20August%202%2C%201990%2C%20at,destroyed%20retreated%20to%20Saudi%20Arabia. Retrieved June 03, 2022.

2. https://journals.sagepub.com/doi/full/10.1177/2347798918812287. Retrieved June 03, 2022.

CHAPTER 1

1. https://www.census.gov/econ/bfs/index.html. Retrieved June 02, 2022.

2. Ibid.

3. https://www.census.gov/econ/bfs/pdf/bfs_current.pdf. Retrieved July 27, 2022.

CHAPTER 2

1. https://www.businessinsider.com/how-many-contacts-does-it-take-before-someone-buys-your-product-2011-7. Retrieved July 21, 2022.

2. Ibid.

3. https://farisalami.medium.com/the-power-of-777-marketing-a8e1a4068479. Retrieved August 1, 2022

CHAPTER 3

1. https://www.finjanshow.com/episodes/the-finjan-show-the-art-of-networking-part-1 . Retrieved August 1, 2022.

2. https://www.finjanshow.com/episodes/the-finjan-show-the-art-of-networking. Retrieved August 1, 2022.

CHAPTER 4

1. https://www.sba.gov/business-guide/plan-your-business/write-your-business-plan. Retrieved August 1, 2022.

2. Ibid.

3. Ibid.

4. https://www.forbes.com/sites/theyec/2021/12/08/a-review-of-the-minimum-viable-product-approach/?sh=7ed59b1c2e20. Retrieved June 02, 2022.

5. https://farisalami.medium.com/setting-long-term-goals-56b6c9f35c67. Retrieved June 02, 2022.

CHAPTER 5

1. https://medium.com/@myISMinc/the-life-cycle-of-a-customer-ed1fa436e9c9. Retrieved August 1, 2022.

2. Ibid.

3. Ibid.

4. Ibid.

5. Ibid.

6. Ibid.

7. Ibid.

8. https://farisalami.medium.com/the-entrepreneurial-mindset-86f1d275a6d5. Retrieved August 1, 2022.

9. Ibid.

CHAPTER 7

1. https://farisalami.medium.com/branding-2e7c9d902103. Retrieved July 27, 2022.

2. https://www.investopedia.com/terms/b/btob.asp. Retrieved June 03, 2022.

3. https://www.entrepreneur.com/article/426600. Retrieved June 02,2022.

4. https://www.entrepreneur.com/article/426600. Retrieved July 22, 2022.

5. https://katanamrp.com/blog/resource-capacity-plan/#:~:text=Product%20capacity%20planning%20ensures%20that,of%20product%20variants%20and%20subassemblies. Retrieved June 02, 2022.

CHAPTER 9

1. https://medium.com/@myISMinc/grow-your-business-with-market-segmentation-151609f64c5. Retrieved August 1, 2022.

2. Ibid.

3. Ibid.

4. https://farisalami.medium.com/market-segments-37dafc977af1. Retrieved July 22, 2022.

CHAPTER 10

1. https://medium.com/@farisalami/understanding-sales-numbers-ac9094f04b2a. Retrieved August, 1, 2022.

CHAPTER 12

1. https://medium.com/@myISMinc/leadership-self-governance-reflection-9694c1ca7a49. Retrieved July 31, 2022.

2. Ibid.

3. https://cdn.advocacy.sba.gov/wp-content/uploads/2022/02/15122206/FinanceFAQ-Final-Feb2022.pdf. Retrieved July 28, 2022.

4. Ibid.

5. Ibid.

6. Ibid.

7. Ibid.

8. https://www.businessnewsdaily.com/4684-technology-terms-for-small-business.html. Retrieved July 27, 2022.

9. https://www.connectingdotsglobally.org/ Retrieved July 28, 2022.

RESOURCES

1. https://www.myisminc.com/ism-programs. Retrieved August 1, 2022.

GLOSSARY

1. https://www.investopedia.com/terms/m/margin.asp#:~:text=In%20business%20accounting%2C%20margin%20refers,of%20goods%20sold%20(COGS). Retrieved June 03, 2022.

2. https://www.investopedia.com/terms/m/margin.asp#:~:text=In%20business%20accounting%2C%20margin%20refers,of%20goods%20sold%20(COGS). Retrieved June 03, 2022.

3. https://www.investopedia.com/terms/m/metrics.asp. Retrieved July 31, 2022.

4. https://www.techtarget.com/searchcustomerexperience/definition/sales-funnel. Retrieved June 03, 2022.

5. https://www.investopedia.com/terms/s/scalability.asp#:~:text=Scalability%2C%20whether%20it%20be%20in,when%20faced%20with%20increased%20production. Retrieved June 03, 2022.

ABOUT THE AUTHOR

As Strategic Management (ISM), Faris Alami works with international leaders and entrepreneurs on strategies and implementation to create an empowering environment for businesses. From startups to established businesses, Faris's years of experience make him a trusted source for business management. Over the course of his career, Faris has been an Entrepreneurial Ecosystem expert with the World Bank, a business advisor with Goldman Sachs 10,000 Small Business Program, and a mentor to MBA students and entrepreneurs globally.

Faris works with high-ranking officials—presidents of countries, ministries, universities, incubators/accelerators, and economic development groups. He also leads the ISM team in supporting entrepreneurs in underserved communities in finding success.

His insights into, strategies for, and facilitation of, entrepreneurship activities have been sought out by more than 100 leaders of nations and organizations.

International Strategic Management's programs include training entrepreneurs, trainers, and management teams in supporting entrepreneurs, and in technology, retail, workforce development, leadership, and culture-related programs.

Faris founded the nonprofit Connecting Dots Globally, a STEMpreneur program in which high school and university students learn to launch a global technology company.

You can find Faris online in several ways:

1. Weekly blog on leadership, entrepreneurship, education, globalization, and community topic

2. Weekly Finjan show podcast on YouTube, Apple podcasts, and other podcasting platforms

3. StartupGrind host

4. Yearly host and keynote speaker of the Global Entrepreneurship Week

5. Guest, live on stage during programs and events, shows and podcasts including international, national, and local news channels, and social media outlets

Current Boards:

- Automation Alley International Center, Advisory Board
- Center for the study Of Citizenship at Wayne State University
- GlobalTies Detroit, Executive Board of Directors/Vice Chair
- Leadership Oakland, Board of Directors
- Franklin University MBA Advisory Board Member
- American Lung Association, Board Member
- Oakland Livingston Human Service Agency Board Member
- George Washington University School of Business Advisory Board Member
- U.S. Global Leadership Coalition Michigan Advisory Committee

Professional Honors and Awards

- Leader of Leaders Award 2019
- Corp! Diversity Business Leader Award 2009

- Professional Resource Business Award 2008
- KNF Appreciation Award 2017
- Global Entrepreneurship Week Host & Keynote Speaker

The Power of Seven in Marketing

FARIS ALAMI

faris.alami@myisminc.com

www.myisminc.com